EXPLORE SEDONA

A Local's Travel Guide to Arizona's Best Hiking, Mountain Biking, Vortexes & Sightseeing

Valentine State Publications

Note: The author receives no compensation for any recommendations or inclusions of any area business in this guide. All reviews and recommendations are based solely on personal experience of the author.

The information contained in this book has been verified to be accurate at the time of publication, but due to the nature of change, the reader should validate all information prior to arriving in Sedona.

"*God created the Grand Canyon, but He lives in Sedona!*"

-Unknown

Contents

View of Twin Buttes from the infamous White Line Trail.

Introduction

Welcome to Sedona! I remember my first introduction to Sedona like it was yesterday: driving up Highway 179 and making that final subtle turn into the Village of Oak Creek, my draw dropping as the gray landscape gave way to the stunning red rocks for which Sedona is known, my first views of Castle Rock, Courthouse Butte, and Bell Rock dominating the landscape. There's something about Sedona that draws you in and holds you captive. In fact, less than 24 hours after first stepping foot into Sedona, my wife and I somehow found ourselves sitting with a real estate agent over lunch and writing an offer for a small condo. We were immediately hooked. Today, Sedona is our second home, and when we're there we aim to maximize our play time and make every moment count. I love to explore; I'm an avid rock climber, hiker, mountain biker, road biker, canyoneer, photographer, and general outdoor enthusiast. This book is really a labor of my love for Sedona, written to help you maximize your own time there in the hopes you will enjoy Sedona as much as my wife and I do!

That said, this book is **not** designed to be an all-encompassing Sedona guide. Plenty of those books exist, and while they're wonderful resources, they can quickly overwhelm you with information of sites you probably don't care to see and trails that just aren't worth it when time is tight. If you'll spend six months per year in Sedona, those resources may be just what you need to see it all, but most people won't spend six months there; they'll spend 3 to 7 nights. My aim with this book is to offer a curated collection of Sedona's best: to cover the heavy-hitters, must-do trails, and must-see attractions for which Sedona is known. The sights in this book will easily keep you busy for two weeks. A large part of my goal is to help you string these together in the most efficient way possible as only a local's advice can. The book is thus grouped into geographic regions and includes tips for linking various activities, as well as sample daily agendas.

Without a doubt, Sedona is paradise, but there's a price to paradise. In Sedona, the steepest price you'll find is heavy traffic and crowds. Especially in the peak season, the road that connects the Village of Oak Creek to Uptown Sedona can back up for miles, making the 6-mile drive take 30-45 minutes or more. This guide will help you minimize your travel between destinations, suggesting activities and restaurants nearby to yours to pair together to maximize trail time and minimize windshield time. Efficiency in this regard benefits not only you, but the entire Sedona community, as traffic is minimized.

Visiting Sedona for the First Time

Airline Travel & Ground Transportation

Most people coming to Sedona by air will arrive at the Phoenix airport, rent a car, and drive themselves to Sedona. There is a shuttle service from Phoenix that can take you to Sedona (groometransportation.com), but unless you're traveling alone and staying for a long time, it's not worth the cost to take the shuttle. The drive is easy and beautiful, and parking in Sedona is easy, trailheads aside. You'll also want a car to get around Sedona since, although there are a few taxi services, Uber and Lyft are non-existent in the area.

The drive from Phoenix airport's rental car center to the Village of Oak Creek is about 2 hours, and it is about 2 hours and 15 minutes to Uptown Sedona. If you're returning on a Sunday afternoon to Phoenix, the traffic can be horrendous . Allow more time to avoid missing your flight. We've made it from the Village in as little as 1 hour and 45 minutes, but we've also had it take 3 hours and 15 minutes. Holidays are the worst times; plan accordingly if you have a flight home to catch.

Sedona is located off I-17, almost a straight shot north of Phoenix. The drive to Sedona is only about 3 or 4 turns once you leave the rental car center: onto the highway in Phoenix, then immediately onto I-17N, then onto 179N into Sedona. It couldn't be much easier. If you're lucky to get a flight into Flagstaff, Arizona, then your drive is even shorter (about 45 minutes). From Flagstaff, you'll also approach Sedona from I-17, but from the north instead of from the south.

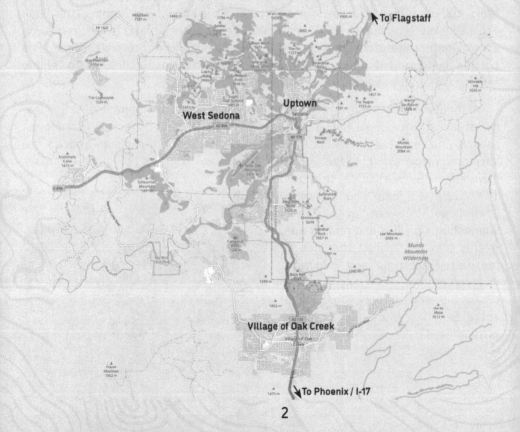

Regions of Sedona

Sedona is a very small town, but being nestled within a national forest divided by mountains and rock formations, it's a bit of a sprawl. Sedona is divided into three main areas: The Village of Oak Creek (Big Park), Uptown, and West Sedona. Each has its own unique characteristics, and choosing where you want to stay is important, as the three locations all have very different vibes.

The Village of Oak Creek is typically the first area you'll come to when approaching from I-17/179N. The Village of Oak Creek is formally named "Big Park" but few, if any, people use that name anymore. It's more known colloquially as "The Village". This area is separated from Uptown by about 5 miles of highway 179, so it's a bit more remote. Despite being the first area you come through from the airport, it's actually the quietest, and it's where most of the locals tend to live. Our condo is in the Village of Oak Creek, and we couldn't be happier with the location we chose. When we return from a busy day on the trail, it's wonderful to have a nice, quiet evening outdoors, away from the throngs of people. In the last few years, quite a bit of commercial development has happened in the Village, including many new fantastic restaurants, cafes, and wine bistros. Despite the quiet ambiance, I promise you won't be longing for meals. There are a few small art galleries, a few shops, some good coffee and pastry places, and a moderately priced grocery store (Clark's Market). You'll find all that you need in the Village if your needs involve a quiet respite.

Uptown Sedona is the smallest region, yet it's what most people think of when they think of Sedona. It's the main hub of activity, with the majority of shops, restaurants, nightlife, and tourists packed into a relatively small area. If you're looking for more energy and excitement, this is the place to stay. You'll be in the middle of everything, which also means shorter average drive times if your destinations tend to be scattered throughout Sedona. Uptown is fun, but very crowded. Expect traffic, tougher parking, longer restaurant waits, and everything else that goes along with locating yourself with the masses.

West Sedona is the final region of Sedona, and as you can expect, it is located to the West of Uptown along Highway 89A. Highway 179 ends in Uptown Sedona, and dumps you onto 89A either towards West Sedona or towards Flagstaff. There are no other roads in or out of Sedona; it's quite a small town! West Sedona is the commercial hub of Sedona, and mixed into the restaurants and shops you'll find banks, grocery stores, realtors, attorneys, schools, and all the typical things that make a town function. You'll also find pharmacies and the UPS Store (useful if you're sending out care packages or shipping gifts), and West Sedona also has a number of residential homes and hotels.

One thing not mentioned above about the three locations is hiking trails. Beautiful hiking is what draws many people to Sedona, and luckily, no matter where you stay, beautiful trails are always nearby. There is no wrong choice of where to stay when it comes to being nearby great trails. Furthermore, keep in mind that while each region has its own personality, Sedona is very small, and the entire Sedona area fits into a circle roughly six to eight miles in diameter (and to be sure, most of that area consists of non-developed wilderness). In the end, it helps to get the most enjoyment out of your trip when you pick your favorite area to stay, but if you can't find availability in your first region, it's very easy to move from area to area. What I will say regarding trails, as a very high-level overview and not an absolute truth, is that the Village has some of the best shorter "must-do" hikes, while West Sedona has some of the longer, more difficult day hikes. Sedona is predominantly a day-hiking city, and if you're looking for epic multi-day adventures, you won't find much. They do exist, but you'll have to look a bit harder and you'll exhaust the supply pretty quickly. But the day hikes in Sedona are simply wonderful. Uptown is a bit of a compromise regarding hikes; there are some nice moderate-distance hikes, a few longer strenuous hikes, and a few shorter, easy hikes. For hiking, rock climbing, and mountain biking, you can't go wrong in any location in Sedona!

Weather / Best Time to Visit

Sedona is a year-round city and can be visited anytime of year with great success, but the best weather is always April to May and September to October. During this time, the average highs are around 80°F, which is cool enough to hike and warm enough to soak in the sun, swim, and relax. Sedona is at a bit of elevation (4,350') and is much cooler than Phoenix but warmer than Flagstaff. Snow occurs most years, but melts away very quickly. Snow in Sedona is a beautiful treat, and you will never regret a visit in the winter. In summer, Sedona can peak in the low 100°s while Phoenix bakes at 115°F, but the dry heat is fairly bearable and there are many hikes that are partially to mostly shaded that can be found just north of Uptown, as well as quite a few swimming holes fed by Oak Creek that are refreshingly cool even on the hottest summer days. Summer does signal monsoon season; a monsoon can be a beautiful event to watch provided you do it safely. Normally dry creek beds can rage, dry canyons flow, and lightning can be pretty epic. Monsoon events are extremely powerful but short lived, and peak between June and August.

Devil's Bridge is much quieter in winter.

Sedona Average Temperatures

	Jan	Feb	Mar	Apr	May	Jun	Jul	Aug	Sep	Oct	Nov	Dec
High	60°	64°	69°	76°	86°	96°	100°	97°	91°	80°	68°	60°
Low	34°	36°	40°	45°	53°	61°	68°	67°	61°	51°	40°	34°

Getting Around

We recommend having a car in Sedona. Uber and Lyft are non-existent in the area, and public transport is limited. A new trailhead shuttle introduced in 2022 has been very successful and is planning expansion. Visit sedonashuttle.com for the latest route maps.

Red Rock Pass Kiosk

Trails aside, most parking in Sedona is free and ample. You will need to pay to park at all hiking trails, and most trails will accept both the Red Rock Pass or a National Parks annual parking pass. The Red Rock Pass can be purchased for $5 per day or $15 per week from any trailhead kiosk, or the annual Red Rock pass can be purchased for $20 from most gas stations and tourism centers.

Notable exceptions that require a dedicated parking pass include Red Rock State Park, Slide Rock State Park, Grasshopper Point, and the West Fork Trail, as well as all national monuments (Tuzigoot, Montezuma's Castle, etc.).

Exploring the Southwest

There is a ton to see and do in Sedona, and you could easily spend a full two weeks here without becoming bored. That said, if it's your first time to Arizona, you may prefer to explore a few different areas during your time here. Sedona is located near many other wonderful places to visit (see the *Outside Sedona* section). Many visitors to Sedona will also visit Flagstaff and Grand Canyon National Park, or spend a day or two in Tucson or Phoenix, drive to Sedona for a few days, continue to Flagstaff for a day, head to the Grand Canyon for a few days, then drive from there to Las Vegas before flying home out of Las Vegas, making a whirlwind 9-day trip of the Southwest. If you have even more time to allocate, you can even continue on to Death Valley, Joshua Tree, Zion, Bryce, or Lake Mead from Las Vegas. The possibilities are quite numerous. Arizona is a large state, though Sedona is centrally located to many wonderful points of interest, and many people come and go without realizing all of the nearby sights to see!

Humphrey's Peak, just up the road in Flagstaff, while a storm is brewing.

Where to Stay

Sedona is divided into three main regions: the Village of Oak Creek (VOC, a quieter location where most locals live), Uptown (the center of the action and shops), and West Sedona (the commercial center). Each location has its advantages, and it's important to remember that Sedona is quite small. Traffic aside, you can drive from the two furthest extremes (West Sedona to VOC) in about 25 minutes.

When choosing where to stay, consider what type of trip you're looking to experience. If you have a strong preference for quiet evenings, stay in VOC. If you want to be in the center of it all, stay in Uptown Sedona. If you have no strong preference here, then the second criteria is to look at your planned activities. If you're in town for a specific activity (film festival, mountain biking, hiking, etc.), it's likely your core activities will be concentrated in one area. Stick to this area to keep it easy. Finally, if you still can't decide, move around! Try a few days in each place if you don't mind a little disruption and unpacking / repacking. We prefer the VOC area, as it has tons of great mountain bike rides and the hikes are shorter, meaning we can crush one out every day over lunch while working our day jobs remotely. When we're on vacation, we tend to prefer the longer hikes of West Sedona.

As far as Airbnb or Vrbo versus hotels, Airbnb's (used here colloquially to mean any private residence rented to you regardless of the platform) are becoming increasingly popular in Sedona, and for good reason. Airbnb's generally offer simple check-in and check-out and come with a host of amenities hotels usually don't offer, like full kitchens. The quality of these listings varies hugely. Look for hosts with good feedback and check the photos carefully! Airbnb is new to Arizona in the last few years (there was previously a statewide ban on rentals shorter than 30 days), so many hosts are still quite new to the business and learning as they go.

Hotels are a safe bet, but generally more expensive and with fewer amenities. You'll get the benefit of daily housekeeping and are more likely to get access to a pool and/or a gym, but in many cases you'll lose the full kitchen you'd get with an Airbnb-type rental. Here's a few hotels, sorted by region, listed from south to north (VOC / Uptown) and east to west (West Sedona):

Village of Oak Creek Hotels

Bell Rock Inn - ★★★☆ - www.sedonahotelsandresorts.com - 6246 Hwy 179

Holiday Inn Express - ★★★☆ - www.ihg.com - 6179 Hwy 179

Sedona Village Lodge - ★★★★☆ - sedonavillagelodge.com - 101 Bell Rock Plaza

The Ridge - ★★★☆ - www.sedonahotelsandresorts.com - 55 Sunridge Cir.

Wildflower Inn at Bell Rock - ★★☆ - wildflowerinnsedona.com - 6086 Hwy 179

Muyawki Inn - ★★☆ - muyawkiinn.com - 6465 Hwy 179

Element Hotel (by Marriott) - ★★★★☆ - www.marriott.com - 6601 Hwy 179

Uptown Hotels

Poco Diablo Resort - ☆☆☆ - www.pocodiablo.com – 1752 Hwy 179

Los Abrigados Resort - ☆☆☆☆ - sedonahotelsandresorts.com - 160 Portal Ln.

Orchards Inn - ☆☆☆☆ - www.orchardsinn.com - 254 N AZ-89A

Amara Resort & Spa - ☆☆☆☆☆ - www.amararesort.com - 100 Amara Ln.

Best Western Arroyo Roble - ☆☆☆☆ - www.bestwestern.com - 400 N AZ-89A

La Petite Sedona - ☆☆ - www.lapetitesedona.com - 500 AZ-89A

West Sedona Hotels

Sky Rock Sedona - ☆☆☆☆ - skyrocksedona.com - 1200 W AZ-89A

Baby Quail Inn - ☆☆☆ - www.babyquailinn.com - 50 Willow Way

Hampton Inn - ☆☆☆☆ - www.hilton.com - 1800 W AZ-89A

The Wilde Resort & Spa - ☆☆☆☆☆ - www.thewilderesort.com - 2250 N AZ-89A

Andante Inn - ☆☆☆ - www.andanteinn.com - 2545 W AZ-89A

Casa Sedona Inn - ☆☆☆☆☆ - www.casasedona.com - 55 Hozoni Dr.

Sedona Summit - ☆☆☆☆ - www.sedonahotelsandresorts.com - 4055 Navoti Dr.

Residence Inn - ☆☆☆☆ - www.marriott.com - 4055 W AZ-89A

Regardless of where you stay, ask for Red Rock views, like this overlook of Sugarloaf Mtn.

Pet Friendly Travel

Most of Sedona is pet-friendly, including trails, many hotels, and even quite a few restaurants. If you're traveling with your canine friend, you'll have plenty of options to choose from to keep both of you busy. The same goes if you're traveling with your cat. Yes, you may actually see leashed cats hiking on the trails. Because, you know, Sedona.

There's a few important considerations when traveling with pets. First, please pick up your pet's waste and carry it with you for proper disposal. We often see people bag their dog poop only to leave the entire bag behind and never come back to retrieve it. Many locations across the country are starting to outright ban pets for this reason, so please don't make Sedona follow suit.

Second, please enjoy the variety of dog-friendly options in town, but understand not every place welcomes dogs. Sedona is unfortunately becoming a mecca for fake service dogs, so please don't be *that* person! Arizona legislation has made it illegal (and with stiff penalties) to misrepresent a pet as a service animal.

Thirdly, consider the time of year and your breed's specific needs. Our little Boston Terrier sits in the condo for most of the summer because the elevation and heat make it too hot for her to be outdoors much of the day. Instead, we rely on evening hikes when the temperature drops. For all dogs, spring and fall are ideal, and for most dogs, winter is also great. Few days see much snow in Sedona.

Almost every trail in Sedona and around Arizona allows dogs when kept under their owner's control on a leash not to exceed 6 feet, but there are a few areas that do not allow dogs at all, or have restrictions. Dogs are NOT welcome at:

- Slide Rock State Park (dogs are allowed in and on trails, but are not allowed at the swim areas, which is the reason most people visit Slide Rock)

- Red Rock State Park

- It's allowed, but not recommended, for most dogs to hike Cathedral Rock or Bear Mountain, as the steep, rocky ascents are difficult for many dogs.

- Grand Canyon State Park (this is not in Sedona of course, but is a nearby spot to hit). Pets are allowed anywhere above the rim but not below the rim.

Sedona also features a dog park, located at 950 Soldiers Pass Rd., which is open until 8:00pm (7:00pm Oct 1 - Apr 1). Collars are required, but leashes are not required in the dog park, and the park does not allow you to bring in dog treats.

Finally, here is a list of hotels and restaurants that are dog friendly, but I always encourage you to call ahead. These things can change as a moment's notice, and it's possible many pet-related restrictions were eased to help drum up new business during the COVID-19 downturn. Phone numbers are provided for your convenience.

Pet-Friendly Hotels:

Many Sedona hotels allow dogs with an added pet fee. Some have restrictions on the size of the pet, or vary the fee based on the size. Many impose limits of two dogs maximum, but others are more lenient. We recommend calling ahead, as some hotels only allow pets in certain classes of room, and this must be reserved ahead of time.

- Sky Ranch Lodge, West Sedona. All dogs, $25/dog/night. (928)-282-6400.
- Arabella Hotel, Uptown. Small breed, $25/dog/night. (855)-649-1200.
- Sedona Village Lodge, VOC. <10 pounds, $25/pet/night, >10 pounds, $40/pet/night. (928) 284-3626.
- El Portal Hotel, Uptown. Up to 3 pets of any size for no fee. (928)-203-9405.
- Poco Diablo Resort, Uptown. All dogs, $30/night fee, must book "pet friendly" room in advance. Not all rooms allow dogs. (928)-282-7333.
- Amara Resort, Uptown. Up to 30 pounds, $50/night, $75/night/two pets. (928)-282-4828.

Pet-Friendly Restaurants:

Sedona restaurants follow regulations set by the county health departments. Namely, dogs are only allowed on outdoor patios where food/drink is not prepared and a separate entrance exists. This non-exhaustive list of restaurants have pet-friendly patios:

- Hideaway House, Uptown. (928)-202-4082.
- Secret Garden Cafe, Uptown. (928)-203-9564.
- Mesa Grill, Uptown/West Sedona. (928)-282-2400.
- Pisa Lisa, West Sedona. (928)-282-5472.
- Open Range Grill, Uptown. (928)-282-0002.
- Creekside Bistro, Uptown. (928)-282-1705.
- 89Agave, Uptown. (928)-282-7200.
- Sedona Pizza Company, Uptown. (928)-203-5656.
- Cucina Rustica, VOC. (928)-284-3010.
- Miley's Cafe, VOC. (928)-284-4123.

Photographing the Desert

Photography is a hobby of mine, and almost all of the images you'll see in this book were captured by me. I'm often asked what gear is best to use for desert photography. I'm also specifically asked about nighttime photography, as Sedona is an International Dark Sky Community. If you haven't seen great starry skies before, then you're in for a real treat in Sedona, especially if you're visiting in summer when the Milky Way band is visible. Make sure you read the *Night Hiking* chapter for more information.

My kit is pretty simple. I shoot a Nikon D750, and often carry my Nikon 24-70 f/2.8 lens. Most of the pictures in this book were shot on that camera with that lens, though a few were shot on my spare body Nikon D90 that I've been known to lug up a rock climbing wall with a tethered bag. Many of the animals and other close-ups in this book were shot on the D750 with a 70-200 f/2.8 lens. Any macros were shot on the 70-200 using Kenko spacer rings to get in very close, and I usually carry a Nikon SB-600 flash or two. I don't carry a dedicated macro lens.

For accessories, I carry the following:

- Polarizing filter (Tiffen brand), important for that Arizona sun

- Graduated neutral density filter (B+W brand), it helps to balance contrast in-camera for the sky versus the rock)

- Carbon fiber monopod (Danger Buddies brand), plus ball head (Manfrotto brand)

- Camera waistpack (Danger Buddies brand), great for rock climbing too!

- Carbon fiber tripod (Manfrotto brand) when shooting at night

- The typical assortment of spare batteries and memory cards (various brands)

Shooting at high noon is tough, though possible. For the most important memories you want to capture, shoot in the early morning or late in the evening during the golden hour. You'll find some of the Arizona sunsets photograph amazingly well. If you must shoot at noon, go for wide landscapes, bracket your shots, and rely on some level of correction in your favorite editing program.

In Sedona, you'll find beauty to photography everywhere. If you're a versatile shooter with many interests, I suggest you try your hand at a bit of everything: astrophotography of the Milky Way, macros of cacti and trees, wide panoramas of the Mogollon Rim, and "normal" 50mm shots of your favorite people on the trails, in the wineries, and on the city streets of Sedona. If you don't have a long lens, don't worry. I find I use my telephoto lens less and less each time I visit Sedona, preferring the 24-70 now for most activities. But if your specific goal is to shoot the many desert animals, you'll want the extra reach a 200mm or longer lens provides. A teleconverter may also be a useful tool for animal photography.

Right: Depth of field can be a concern with longer lenses, but the desert isn't lacking for sunlight so you can really stop down your aperture if you need more depth of field.

Left: Landscapes are best when stopped down to f/8 or higher to make sure everything is crisp and sharp.

Right: A simple, no-frills shot of the trailhead sign at the start of each hike helps you remember where you took each picture. After a while, they all blend together!

Below: You don't need a special lens to get great cactus shots. A monopod helped with this shot taken with a 24-70 zoomed all the way in and shot at f/11.

Wildlife Viewing

If you're not used to the desert, it's likely you'll find the Arizona wildlife to be quite unique and, in some cases, a little creepy or even downright scary (check out the Tarantula Hawk Wasp sometime on Google; it's the stuff of nightmares). But for the most part, Sedona animals are harmless to humans and generally reclusive and fun to observe. Even the tarantulas and scorpions are interesting to see, and sightings of the former are quite rare on the overused trails these days.

If you're looking for animals, late spring is a great time to visit. The weather isn't too hot, the monsoons have just started (which provide all animals with much-needed water), and the desert is still in-bloom. Winter is the least ideal time for most animal sightings; not only are sightings a bit more rare, but you'll be less comfortable waiting in the cold to see them.

The desert sun is quite punishing to many mammals, so you'll also want to do your sightseeing in the earlier morning hours, dusk hours, or even in the later evening when the sun has fully set and darkness reigns. The exception here is the reptiles; the many lizards on the trail are best spotted in full daylight, as they seem to rather enjoy the sun, and can often be seen basking on rocks, doing their push-ups as you approach.

As far as where to go to see the various animals, the best place for sightings are typically at known watering holes, especially for larger mammals like deer, coyotes, and javelinas. Slide Rock State Park, Page Springs Hatchery (not in Sedona but nearby in the Cornville area), Red Rock State Park, or other points along Oak Creek are all great choices. Hiking trails that pass water are also good choices, like West Fork Trail and Templeton Trail, but heavy use by hikers on these trails makes early morning or evening the best times to spot wildlife. The peak hiking hours will scare most animals away. The lizards and birds are everywhere; you'll have no problem sighting these along the trails as you hike, regardless of crowds. Tarantulas and snakes are a luck-of-the-draw, and sightings along trails are somewhat rare. Scorpions are only observed at night and usually with the aid of a ultraviolet light, which makes them glow impressively in a way that they can't be missed (see the image to the right).

Photographing animals is best done with a long zoom lens. I prefer a 70-200 f/2.8, which gives me the reach I need and the wide aperture that helps freeze the otherwise fast motion of animals. Stop down your aperture just a little; f/4 on a f/2.8 lens usually is a good compromise between extreme sharpness and eliminating motion blur.

In the end, animal sightings take a bit of luck over time. We've been coming to Sedona for over 4 years and have yet to see some of the animals we've been hoping to photograph. But that's okay, as it gives us a reason to come back for another visit (as if we needed one)!

Right: A smattering of the various things in Sedona that all want to eat you! Keep a healthy distance from all wildlife, and don't disturb them just for the sake of your photo, no matter how tempting it may be!

Vortex Energy - Exploring Sedona's Vortexes

Sedona is rumored to contain multiple vortex energy fields (in fact, all of Sedona is itself an energy vortex). Vortices, or vortexes as they're called colloquially, are areas of energy entering or exiting the earth, the former being feminine vortexes and the latter being masculine. These vortexes are believed to have spiritual, psychological, and physical healing powers and are known to increase energy and tranquility.

Sedona is not the only place on earth claimed to have vortexes; other global sites include Machu Picchu and Stonehenge. Domestically, similar energy sites are reported at Mount Shasta in California and Crater Lake in Oregon, though Sedona is arguably the most well known location for vortexes in the United States.

In Sedona, there are four major vortex sites that can be hiked. You won't find much in the way of signage directing you, but fortunately these hikes are all well established trails. Hiking these vortexes will invigorate you, destress you, and bring a sense of energy and accomplishment to your day. Whether that's due to the vortex energy itself or simply the byproduct of exercise and fresh air is for you to decide! Many of these hikes are also listed under the *Hiking* chapter, while the focus here is on the spiritual awareness these hikes are reported to offer.

Bell Rock Vortex ♂ 🕐 1hr 📍 ~0.8 mile round trip

Bell Rock is a site of masculine energy (energy exiting the earth, reported to improve your serenity and energy). Skip the Bell Rock Pathway trailhead and proceed directly to the Courthouse Vista parking lot. Follow the trail straight up to the base of Bell Rock and follow the signs marked "Bell Rock Climb" as high as your comfort allows. You cannot gain this iconic summit by hiking alone. The easiest approach to the very top requires a technical roped rock climb on your own gear, but you can definitely make it about 80% of the way either by scrambling straight up the large northern bowl, or more safely by the obvious roundabout trail that cuts left of the formation to a series of ledges. It's not necessary to reach the summit to feel the power of the vortex. You'll begin to feel energized as soon as you step onto the rocks that define the base of Bell Rock. If you make it up the water streaked bowl, you'll be treated to a very large ledge where you can relax for a bit of meditative contemplation. The photo here of the juniper tree was shot from this ledge; it's reported the twisting of juniper tree branches is due to the spiraling vortex energy.

Cathedral Rock Vortex

♂ ♀ 🕐 1hr 📍 1.2 miles round trip

Cathedral Rock consists predominantly of masculine energy in the lower portion of the hike, yielding to a combination of masculine and feminine energy towards the top and the saddle (the point between the two main rock pillars and the traditional end of the trail). I personally know rock climbers who claim to have sensed the vortex energy in the form of vibrations even at the top of The Mace (one of the leftmost pillars), though I have never felt it myself. I do get a sense of vigor every time I hike this spot, and it's easy to slip into a trance-like state at the end of the trail while gazing at the overlook. This hike is short and steep, so take your time and take in the views!

Above: Cathedral Rock, one of the most visited vortexes.

Airport Mesa

♂ ⏱ 1.5hr 📍 3.2 miles round trip

A rocky loop trail around Sedona's regional airport, this mesa is also home to one of Sedona's strongest masculine energy vortexes, and even if you can't immediately feel the energy of this vortex, you'll see it evidenced by the numerous twisted juniper trees along the trail.

Park in the angled lot part of the way up Airport Rd. or in the private lot at the end of Airport Rd. ($3 fee, Red Rock pass not accepted). If you're in the airport lot, hike down Sedona View Trail to the Airport Loop Trail. Before turning either direction onto the 3.2-mile loop trail, head up to the overlook point for a breathtaking panoramic view of Sedona. This overlook is a wonderful spot to enjoy a sunset, absorb the vortex energy, and stargaze over the city.

From the overlook, begin your main vortex adventure by turning either direction onto the Airport Loop Trail, then enjoy 3.2 miles of beautiful, exposed hiking around the mesa. For much of the hike, you'll be hiking along fairly exposed cliff side, but the hiking is easy and invigorating. A side trail (Table Top Trail) continues on to a nearby knoll. Table Top Trail is located roughly halfway along the length of Airport Loop Trail, making it an ideal rest spot where you can kick back and watch the aircraft coming and going from the airport before continuing on the rest of the way around the mesa.

The best time to hike the Airport Mesa vortex is spring and fall, but summer evenings can be pleasant as well, and this area tends to be exposed to a good amount of wind to help keep you cool.

Hot air balloons visible from the Airport Mesa vortex overlook.

Boynton Canyon

♂ ♀ 🕐 4hr ⚲📍7.3 miles round trip

   Boynton Canyon, the home of the famous Subway Cave, Native American cliff dwelling remains and spiritual sites, and the Kachina Tree Cave, is also home to one of Sedona's most powerful vortexes, one that combines both masculine and feminine energy together. This is certainly no secret, and this easy hike, approachable to all, often yields many fun people soaking in a little bit of the vortex energy. I've seen flautists playing on top of rocks, yogis galore, and of course, many tour groups coming to soak in a little bit of their own vortex energy.

   This wonderful trail has beautiful scenic vistas at the start, turning into a dense forest as the trail progresses. Boynton Canyon is a box canyon, meaning it has a true dead-end at the canyon walls, and it's at this point the vortex energy reaches it's peak, so be sure to take the trail right to the end. It's a hike you won't regret!

   The best time to hike Boynton Canyon vortex is really anytime. The start of the hike can be warm in the summer as it's quite exposed, but as the hike turns to forest, you'll gain a respite from the desert sun under the canopy of trees. In winter, start a bit later so the sun has risen above the canyon walls for warmth. An early start, on the other hand, can often reveal beautiful morning frost on all of the leaves, which is truly a stunning sight that adds to the beauty of the hike. If you're even luckier, you'll be treated to a gentle blanket of snow on the red rocks, a site that's truly amazing, though catch it quick because it never sticks around for long!

A cold winter day is a great time to visit the Boynton Canyon vortex. It keeps crowds down, creates frosty beauty, like on the tips of this Manzanita, and the cold air in your lungs is truly invigorating!

Hiking

Sedona is a day-hiker's paradise, with hikes ranging from under a mile to ones taking about half a day to complete. The hikes in this book are grouped by region within Sedona: the Village, Uptown and points north, and West Sedona. This can help you to group hikes in similar locations together so you can string a few back-to-back with minimal driving.

Some Sedona hikes have short sections of scrambles (areas requiring hands and feet to climb), and these are highlighted. Any hikes that have Class 3 or 4 scrambles are listed under the *Technical Hikes* section (see the *Scrambling Guide* below). Class 1 and 2 is considered "normal" hiking.

Icon Guide:

Trailhead GPS Coordinates

Round-Trip Distance / Grade

Approximate Hiking Time

Crowd Level / Popularity

View Rating (1-5 Stars)

Cell Signal (Verizon / AT&T)

Favorite Local Restaurant

Best Season to Hike

Scrambling Guide:
Class 1: An exposed hike with easy walking but perhaps along a steep cliff. Low risk.
Class 2: Steeper, with occasional use of hands & moderate exposure but fairly low risk.
Class 3: Hands & feet required. A rope may be desired & falls may cause injury.
Class 4: Hard scrambling to very easy rock climbing with potentially fatal falls.
Class 5: Rock climbing; technical ascending with a rope & climbing gear.

Sedona elevation is about 4,300' above sea level, with the tallest common peaks in Sedona stretching to about 7,100'. If you are coming from sea level, prepare to feel the elevation a little, but it's nothing like what you'd feel in the Rockies or other higher elevation ranges. Most people adapt in a day or two. Stay hydrated to help acclimate yourself to the heat. The desert sun is quite intense, and you'll need to drink more than you think to stay hydrated.

Most Sedona area hikes are quite short, so you can venture off into the wilderness with minimal gear and return to your car to restock before the next hike. Each hike description also lists our favorite nearby restaurant for a post-hike drink or meal.

Some hikes are quite crowded. Please maintain good etiquette, even if others don't. We've included some tips on the next page as a reminder of what to wear, bring, expect, and how to be a good steward of the trail while exploring Sedona.

Hiking Tips & Etiquette

General Considerations

Hiking in Sedona is quite easy, at least logistically. There's abundant trails that lead to just about anywhere you want to go, and you can find the perfect level of difficulty from the flat path of Bell Rock Pathway to the steepest mountainsides like Bear Mountain and Wilson Mountain.

There's a few things to be aware of when hiking in Sedona. First, you're hiking in the desert; it's hot, dry, and sunny in summer with temperatures up to 100°F in June through August. In winter, snow is possible in December through February, though it tends to melt away quite rapidly. In any season, take lots of water with you. Dehydration can sneak up on you because the dryness makes it feel like you're not sweating. Believe me, you are, it just evaporates instantly. Eventually, you're fatigued, confused, and struggling to progress on the trail. Stay hydrated!

The elevation in Sedona is modest at 4,350', with Wilson Mountain (Sedona's highest peak) clocking in at 7,122'. For those visiting from lower elevations, Sedona's elevation is not high enough to cause much concern for your breathing during a routine hike. The thinner, dry air does promote very rapid sunburn, however, so apply suntan lotion liberally!

As far as footwear for hiking, I personally prefer to always hike Sedona in a pair of approach shoes. For those not familiar with this shoe style, it's an intermediate style between a sneaker and a rock climbing shoe, with a generous covering of rubber over the toes for protection, but lacking the stability and padding (and weight) of a hiking shoe. I find a full-blown hiker is generally unnecessary, but a sneaker is sometimes too lightweight for a full day of hiking (and does not grip the rocks as well). For those who enjoy scrambling, approach shoes also let you tackle the 4th-Class quite easily. They stick to the slickrock wonderfully.

Multi-Use Trails

Many Sedona trails are open to hiking, mountain biking, and horseback riding. Inside the US Forest Service's designated wilderness boundaries, mountain bikes are not allowed, so if you are bothered by bikes on the trail, stick to those hikes in the wilderness. Otherwise, be aware that bikes are welcome on most trails in Sedona. Bikers are supposed to yield to everyone. Hikers always yield to those on horseback, and hikers moving downhill always yield to other hikers moving uphill.

Horses always have the right of way. You'll see these pictured yield signs everywhere as a common reminder of this. When approaching oncoming horses, position yourself

on the downhill side of the horse, and the lead rider will give you instructions. If approaching from the rear, announce yourself quickly in a friendly manner. Don't "silently stalk" the group waiting for a chance to pass, as this may spook the horses. It's better to announce yourself as you approach.

Stay On-Trail

The desert is a fragile yet durable environment. The various flora and fauna in this region have developed adaptations to enable survival in these harsh conditions, though humans can very quickly destroy this balance. One easily appreciates how a cactus may store water to survive a drought, but not many people appreciate how the very ground you walk on has been shaped by evolution.

Called cryptobiotic crust, the ground you walk on in Sedona contains organisms (lichen, moss, and bacteria) that form a protective layer over the ground that helps retain nutrients and prevent erosion so plants and animals can survive better. You won't find this on-trail (the wear and tear destroys the crust), but that's OK on-trail because the forest service (and many volunteers) help to maintain the trails. But when you step off-trail, and "Bust the Crust," you destroy literally hundreds of years of growth of this unique and special life that is not possible to restore. Stick to established trails. For the few adventures (climbs and scrambles) I'll list here, these follow established spur trails, so stick to those and the listed GPS coordinates and resist the urge to bushwhack.

Leave No Trace

Simply stated, please don't leave your trash on the trails (including your dog's poop, bagged or not). Please pack out everything you take in. Most trailheads have waste disposal. Go one step further when possible and pick up any trash you see on or around the trails. Also avoid building your own cairns on the trail, as this leads to increased erosion and can confuse other hikers and lead them off trail.

Most importantly, don't carve or deface rocks, and don't let your children do it. The red rocks of Sedona are formed from the slow oxidation of iron in the rock. When you carve or scratch this thin later, even gently, it can take many, many years to heal and re-oxidize.

Miscellaneous Tips

Trail counters like this one are popping up everywhere in Sedona. Don't worry when you see these; they're not cameras, and they're not spying on you! The US Forest Service sets these up to monitor trail use for various studies and to determine how to allocate trail maintenance dollars. Just ignore these and move on!

Finally, if you see Forest Service workers or private volunteers working on the trails while you're out hiking or biking, please take a second and say thank you! The hike you're enjoying wouldn't be possible without them and the thousands of hours that have been put in to maintain these wonderful trails.

A quiet hike with little shade and many interesting geological features, Turkey Creek Trail follows a dry creek past Turkey Domes and Turkey Tank before ascending House Mountain.

Turkey Creek Trail

📍 34.809580, -111.817833

📏 5.9mi, Difficult

🕐 3 Hours

👣 Not Crowded

🔭 ☆☆☆☆

📶 <30% Coverage

🍴 Tortas de Fuego

❄ Winter - Spring

Turkey Creek Trail is often overlooked by many hikers due to a short length of rugged road you'll need to drive off of Verde Valley School Rd. If you're not comfortable with the off-road drive, park earlier and walk; it's a short approach to the trailhead. Geologically speaking, this hike has it all. You'll follow a dry riverbed and wind past Turkey Domes (which also offer some multi-pitch rock climbs), you'll pass Turkey Tank, and if you know where to look, you'll even pass a massive sinkhole located at GPS: 34.802778, -111.823893. The sinkhole opening is slightly off-trail and only about 5' across, but underground it expands to an opening of 25' x 85' at a depth of approximately 80'. The sinkhole is neat to see, but please don't attempt to cross the Forest Service's barrier, you'll disturb the bats that roost in the sinkhole. To top this hike off (pun intended), this otherwise fairly flat and easy hike finishes with a brief yet steep non-technical ascent up House Mountain, an old dormant volcano. When you arrive at the House Mountain saddle (where most people end their hike), take a small narrow trail (seldom used, and route finding may be needed) that will take you beyond to the basalt summit, where beautiful panoramic views over the Verde Valley await!

View from House Mountain peak.

The Crack (Bell Trail)

📍 34.674272, -111.713474

🏃📍 7mi, Easy

🕐 2 Hours

🐾 Moderately Crowded

🔭 ☆☆☆

📶 <10% Coverage

🍴 Miley's Cafe

❄️ Summer

A popular swimming hole and cliff jumping spot on Wet Beaver Creek, The Crack's lengthy approach cuts down on crowds, though this swimming hole can still be a large party in the summertime.

Cliff jumping & trout fishing - the perfect day!

Not to be confused with Bell Rock (which is unrelated), Bell Trail is the access trail for The Crack, though the trail continues mostly unused for another 4 miles past The Crack.

Bell Trail is hot and sunny in summer, but summer is the best time to swim in Sedona's famous cliff jumping spot. The long approach makes this swimming hole quieter than Slide Rock, but not by much. The length of the trail disperses the sightseers, but The Crack itself is usually very crowded and can sometimes be an all-out party. That said, it's still a very suitable place to bring children, provided they can complete the long approach in the heat.

Park at the Bell Trailhead on Hwy 618 south of I-17. If parking is full, use the newer Bruce Brockett Trailhead to park (GPS: 34.678947, -111.717238), which connects directly into the Bell Trail. Follow the well-worn trail 3.5 miles to The Crack. The trail is quite easy until the steeper descent right at the end, so even in the hottest days of summer, it's never unbearably tough. Bring plenty of water, and consider a fishing pole if you're an expert angler - you'll find good trout fishing at various spots along the creek. Adventurous hikers can follow the 7.7-mile Bell Trail well past The Crack and connect into other various trails to complete a loop, but few people do so.

This is a secluded hike through a wide canyon that follows a normally dry creek bed with beautiful trees and offers scenic vistas, red rock views, and our favorite part, cows!

Woods Canyon Trail

📍 34.756426, -111.763233

📍 7mi, Difficult

🕐 3 Hours

🐾 Not Crowded

👓 ☆☆☆

📶 20% Coverage

🍴 Dellepiane Burger

❄ Spring - Fall

Start this hike from the Red Rock Ranger Station on Hwy 179 south of the Village of Oak Creek. One of the closest Sedona area hikes as you approach from Phoenix, this hike actually sees very little foot traffic given its location, perhaps because the start is not the most scenic compared to others in the area. It starts on a jeep road through a cattle field before entering the mouth of the canyon, which very slowly narrows, but never turns into a true narrow canyon. The second half of the hike is quite pretty as you pass the dry stream bed and the many trees growing from within.

Along the hike, you'll pass cattle, rattlesnakes, birds aplenty, and the occasional deer as you make your way deeper into the canyon. There is a "typical" ending to the trail at the 3.5 mile mark along the dry creek bed pictured below, but adventurous hikers can press on through the rest of the canyon. Note, during the monsoon season, Woods Canyon is best avoided.

Woods Canyon can also be linked with the Hot Loop Trail (confusingly, although Hot Loop is quite hot, it's not actually a loop, so be prepared for a long out-and-back hike to the top of Horse Mesa). These two trails are frequented by overnight hikers.

You'll be treated to a gorgeous view of the dry creek bed for a beautiful ending to this canyon.

Transept Trail

📍 34.790480, -111.792833

⛰ 6.5mi, Moderate

🕐 3 Hours

✊ Not Crowded

🔭 ☆☆☆

📶 20% Coverage

🍴 Butterfly Burger

❄ Winter - Spring

A newer trail, Transept Trail still isn't on many maps, which helps keep crowds at bay. This trail offers an alternate approach to the HiLine and Cathedral Rock Trails from the south of the VOC.

If you seek solitude on a busy day, Transept Trail may be exactly what you're looking for. Parking for this trail is at an unpaved lot on Verde Valley School Rd. The trail starts across the road with a fairly aggressive uphill climb but is otherwise an easy to moderate trail to hike. You'll be treated to beautiful overlooks of the red rock scenery in the Verde Valley School Rd. area, Castle Rock (which is the first Sedona rock formation you'll see when you approach via Phoenix), House Mountain, and the back of Cathedral Rock. You can actually hike to the end of the Cathedral Rock Trail from the Transept Trail. It's a much longer approach and skips the entirety of the Cathedral Rock hike, but with that you'll bypass the crowds and crowded parking area. Take Transept to the HiLine, hang a left onto the HiLine, and when you see a sign on the HiLine pointing out a sharp left turn in the trail on a rock face, continue on a very obvious hiker's spur trail (GPS: 34.813695, -111.787081). Follow the easy spur trail to a short Class 2 scramble up the backside of Cathedral Rock to the ending saddle. This is a more peaceful way to hike to Cathedral Rock's most scenic viewpoint, but it clocks in at about 8 miles round-trip, making it much more committing than the usual 1.2-mile hike from the Cathedral Rock Trail parking lot.

Scenic views of Cathedral Rock from its less popular side, seen from Transept Trail.

A short loop offering access to Templeton Trail and Oak Creek, Buddha Beach, and Crescent Moon Ranch, Baldwin Trail offers beautiful open views of Cathedral Rock and the Village of Oak Creek.

Baldwin Trail

📍 34.821736, -111.808032

📍 2.6mi, Easy

🕐 1.5 Hours

🐾 Moderately Crowded

🔭 ☆☆☆☆☆

📶 50% Coverage

🍴 Rotten Johnny's Pizza

☀ All Year

Take Verde Valley School Rd. until the gravel ends, and then continue to the large paved parking lot. Baldwin Trail is a fairly easy loop that you can hike in either direction. Starting with a left onto the trail from the parking lot (clockwise on a map) is recommended, however, as it's more scenic and you connect to other trails and Oak Creek more quickly if that's your goal. Nearby the creek, you can also explore Red Rock Crossing (this spur trail is where you'll get the classic photo of Cathedral Rock with Oak Creek running in front of it, shown above. Afternoons are better if this is your goal). Just past this crossing is the turnoff for Templeton Trail, which follows Oak Creek through the forest before becoming quite steep and heading up to meet Cathedral Rock Trail in time for the most fun parts (translation: Class 2 scramble) up to the Cathedral Rock ending saddle. These two options aside, Baldwin is a great trail when hiked on its own, and you'll be perfectly content to hike the loop and enjoy beautiful vista views. Baldwin Trail is also a popular spot for horseback riding, so it's likely you'll see individuals or groups of riders. Remember, hikers always yield to horses; follow the instructions of the lead horse rider, which usually will be to step to the downhill side of the trail while the horses pass.

Baldwin Trail offers quick access to Oak Creek via a short side-trip on Templeton Trail.

Bell Rock Pathway

📍 34.791277, -111.761929

🚶 3mi, Easy

🕐 1.5 Hours

👣 Moderately Crowded

🔭 ☆☆☆☆☆

📶 100% Coverage

🍴 Pisa Lisa (VOC)

📅 All Year

The large bell-shaped rock when you enter the VOC is none other than Bell Rock! One of the easiest hikes in the area, an optional sustained scramble up the face makes for a more adventurous hike.

Interestingly, Bell Rock Pathway is not the fastest route to Bell Rock itself, but it does lead past the formation and continues for a few miles to the intersection with the Little Horse Trail. Unless you're intentionally combining it with Little Horse which makes a wonderful longer hike, I recommend you hike around the formation, to the start of the Bell Rock Climb, then continue on to the Rector Connector, a new and much quieter trail that circumnavigates Bell Rock before leaving you on Big Park Loop. From here, you can either bee-line back to the car or extend into a longer easy hike past Courthouse Butte, eventually looping back to your car.

If you're looking for the approach up the face of Bell Rock, skip the Bell Rock Trailhead, park at Courthouse Vista, and start on Bell Rock Pathway from there. Just keep walking towards the rock and follow the well-marked path of Forest Service cairns. You'll basically walk right up the face of the rock. A small bowl on the north side is a short Class 3 scramble, or a slightly longer path to the left of the bowl skirts the edge and ascends as a Class 2 scramble. It's not possible to summit the rock proper without ropes and technical gear; the easiest summit route is a 5.8 climb.

Bell Rock is one of the most iconic rock formations in Sedona.

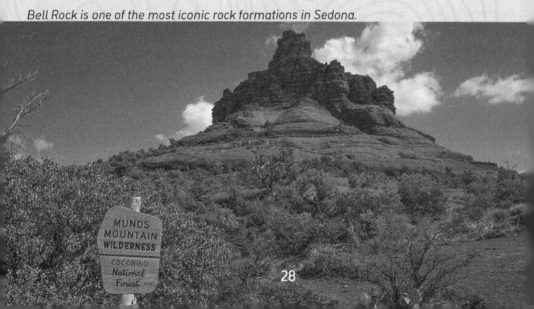

Courthouse Butte is Bell Rock's next-door neighbor, and the two are often visited together. Courthouse Butte is larger, and the hike around the formation is significantly longer but worth it.

Courthouse Butte

📍 34.805929, -111.766478

📍 3mi, Easy

🕐 1.5 Hours

✊ Moderately Crowded

🔭 ☆☆☆☆☆

📶 100% Coverage

🍴 Tortas de Fuego

🎇 All Year

Park at Courthouse Vista. Start left on Bell Rock Pathway to the junction with Llama Trail. You may want to stop at Baby Bell on the way; follow the signs, and a very short Class 2 gains you the top of Baby Bell. You can connect back to Llama from Baby Bell. Turn right on Llama until it briefly intersects Courthouse Butte Loop, one of the few trails in the VOC where mountain bikes are not allowed.

Follow Courthouse Butte Loop around the majority of the formation, soaking in the views of the massive rock structure as you go. The trail will turn into Big Park Loop on the south side of the formation, which also traces along the southern side of the rock before turning towards the VOC and the intersection of Bell Rock Trail, which will take you back to the parking lot (or you can take the Rector Connector and pass between Bell Rock and Courthouse Butte to complete the true loop around Courthouse). As an aside, the Rector Connector is one of our favorite places to view scorpions. Don't worry, you'll only see them at night, and usually only with a UV light.

If you want to summit Courthouse Butte, see the *Technical Ascent* section.

Above: Bell Rock and Courthouse Butte in summer. Below: Courthouse Butte in winter.

Little Horse Trail

⚲ 34.824231, -111.775766

🏃 3mi, Moderate

🕐 1.5 Hours

🐾 Moderately Crowded

🔭 ☆☆☆

📶 100% Coverage

🍴 Hideaway House

📅 All Year

Offering a moderate hike finishing at Chicken Point with views of Twin Buttes, this is a great spot at sunset, as it's easy to night-hike out with a lamp.

Park at the Little Horse lot on 179's east side north of the Courthouse Vista parking lot and south of the rotary with Back O' Beyond and Indian Cliffs Rd.

Begin on Bell Rock Pathway for about half a mile before turning left and descending into a wash. Head left in the wash and exit right after a few hundred feet. The trail will ascend until reaching the junction with the Llama Trail. At this point, it'll mostly flatten out for the rest of the walk around Twin Buttes before starting a smaller final climb to Chicken Point. The Llama Trail takes you towards Baby Bell Rock, Bell Rock, and Courthouse Butte, and though it's beautiful, it's not the prize of this hike; continue on Little Horse to Chicken Point.

At Chicken Point, you'll be treated to great views but also a constant stream of Pink Jeeps. Little Horse Trail turns into Broken Arrow Trail, continuing on past Devil's Dining Room sinkhole, or you can take the split from Broken Arrow to High on the Hog. You can hike a full circle around Twin Buttes, though it will involve some on-road walking. To do this, take Broken Arrow to High on the Hog, connecting into Hog Heaven, then take a left onto Pig Tail. Follow Pig Tail to Mystic Trail, take a left onto Mystic, then follow it back to Chapel Rd. Take a left on Chapel Rd. (now is a great opportunity to actually visit the Chapel of the Holy Cross, as when you're on foot you'll skip the parking struggles). As the road starts to ascend steeply on its final approach to the chapel, a small parking lot on the right hides a trailhead onto Chapel Trail, which leads back to Little Horse just before the final approach to Chicken Point.

One of Sedona's most elusive creatures, the Pink Jeep is a shy and docile creature, and only comes out once every four minutes between 8am and 6pm. Please do not feed the jeeps; let's keep these majestic creatures wild.

Seriously though, these tours are fun, and Pink Jeep is one of the largest donors to trail maintenance in Sedona. So, that's cool.

Cathedral Rock Trail is a "must-do" hike known for its vortex energy and ascends to the base of the iconic rock formation.

Cathedral Rock Trl.

 34.825330, -111.788624

1.2mi, Moderate

1 Hour

Highly Crowded

☆☆☆☆☆

100% Coverage

Javelina Cantina

All Year

Park in the lot about a mile down Back O' Beyond Rd., centrally located between the Village and Uptown. Do not park on the road! This is one of the more popular hikes in the area, and arguably the worst for parking. This is a great opportunity to use the new free trailhead shuttles!

This trail logs 1.2 miles round-trip and is moderate to difficult due to a 40' section of Class 2 scrambling up an exposed rock face. Use caution or a spotter, but don't be deterred; small footholds have been carved into the rock, and we've seen children, dogs, and plenty of people make it safely and securely. After the Class 2 scramble, the steep ascent continues right up to the end of the trail, but the hiking is moderate and non-technical. When you reach the end, enjoy beautiful views looking out over Baldwin Trail. It's a great sunset spot and a perfect place for wedding photos! The small ledge to the right looks narrow and sketchy, but it's actually quite wide, so definitely check it out.

For an added boost of adrenaline, hike this at night with a UV light and headlamp; it's a great place to check out scorpions when the weather is warm enough, or to stargaze or photograph the Milky Way on a warm summer's eve!

Are we there yet? Yes.

Right: A Class-2 scramble on Cathedral Rock may require hands and feet to ascend. Though the passage is easy, the risk of injury is real! If in doubt, ask for a spot!

31

Also known as Raven Caves, this short hike to a cave system near Uptown also offers access to Oak Creek for a nice respite from the Sedona sun.

Sedona Caves

📍 34.841956, -111.776347

🧭 0.5mi, Easy

🕐 1 Hour

🐾 Not Crowded

👀 ☆☆☆

📶 100% Coverage

🍴 Mooney's Irish Pub

❄️ Spring - Fall

Park in the small unmarked lot at the GPS coordinates listed above. If coming from the south, make a U-turn on 179 just north of the GPS coordinates (at Oak Creek Cliffs Dr.) because you will need to be in the southbound lane to access the parking lot. It only holds about 5 cars, making this a very quiet hike.

Follow the obvious trail about 1/4 mile one-way to the cave system. Explore the caves, but use caution. The passage from cave to cave is exposed on a cliff-side. For those seeking shelter from the sun, the caves are a great outing, and the round-trip hike can be done in much less than one hour, including some time to explore the caves. For those seeking a dip in the river, follow the steep but well-worn trail down to Oak Creek, toss a towel on the large rocks, and relax the day away! This is one of our favorite spots to hang a hammock on a hot sunny day, since we can hide away in the shade!

This should go without saying, but please don't deface the cave rocks or add graffiti to the cave.

Above: Oak Creek provides a wonderful summer oasis. Right: View from inside the cave. Look carefully and you can see my wife waving hello from another cave on the right! Below: The cave is a great spot for photos!

Broken Arrow Area

📍 34.845539, -111.757014

🏞 3-5mi, Moderate

🕐 1.5 - 2.5 Hours

🐾 Moderately Crowded

🔭 ☆☆☆☆☆

📶 100% Coverage

🍴 Hideaway House

❄ All Year

Broken Arrow Trail takes you to the same destination as Little Horse (Chicken Point, pictured below), but approaches it from the north. Broken Arrow is a nice trail, but the best trails in the area are those that cross Broken Arrow, including the "Pig" trails such as High on the Hog, Hog Heaven, Pigtail, and Peccary. Random fact: a peccary is a javelina, and Sedona is crawling with them. Despite a similar appearance to a pig, there is absolutely no genetic relationship. Javelinas aren't pigs at all!

Start at the Broken Arrow Trailhead on Morgan Rd., and you will quickly come to a junction on a large rock face. Broken Arrow will turn leftish while to the right you can follow Hog Wash Trail. Taking Hog Wash around the north side of Twin Butte (the large rock formation in front of you) is a nice option. You'll trace the edges of this formation before turning onto Peccary and finally Pigtail. Pigtail is a very fast one-way downhill mountain bike ride; you'll be facing approaching bikes so keep an eye out. Follow Pig Tail back to Hog Wash, and Hog Wash to Hog Heaven. Hog Heaven becomes a fairly exposed hike, but those timid of heights will still feel comfortable; the hiking is easy, and the scenery is great.

When Hog Heaven meets Twin Butte, you can either take the shorter approach to your car (Twin Butte) or continue on to High on the Hog. The former descends near to the trailhead, while the latter continues up and meets Broken Arrow Trail not far from Chicken Point, meaning you can finish the path to Chicken Point, double back, continue back down Broken Arrow, pass the large sinkhole for a quick inspection, and then return to your car. If you choose the recommended loop, expect about a 5-mile hike.

Sunset at Chicken Point can be quite dramatic.

One of Sedona's must-do hikes, the West Fork of Oak Creek is truly a unique hike paralleling and crossing the creek and meandering through forests as you wind your way up the canyon. Most hikers stop when wet feet become mandatory, but for adventurous hikers, it turns into a beautiful slot canyon that can be followed for miles and even completed as an overnight excursion.

Park in the West Fork Trail parking lot on N AZ-89A (8.8 miles north of Midgley Bridge). Note that the Red Rock Pass is not accepted here, and a $10 day-use fee applies. This parking lot fills up quickly, and this hike is fairly crowded. Due to the length of the hike, however, the crowds usually disperse nicely, making the trail peaceful and uncrowded.

West Fork Trail

📍 34.990569, -111.742798

📏 6.4mi, Moderate

🕐 2.5 Hours

Moderately Crowded

👓 ☆☆☆☆☆

📶 Minimal Coverage

🍴 Mago Café

❄ Summer / Fall

This trail starts across a bridge and past some Native American ruins, then enters the forest and crosses Oak Creek quite a few times. The crossings are quite easy, as stones and other natural objects are strategically placed to facilitate a dry crossing. This canyon feels unlike most other hikes in the area and is teeming with life. It's not uncommon to see birds, snakes, small fish, and other signs of wildlife not usually observed in the Uptown Sedona deserts.

This hike is not technical, though once past the "typical" ending it can get slightly technical, with mandatory wading in waist-deep water. Although the standard hike can be enjoyed much of the year, it's the watery ending that make this hike best reserved for summer when the cold waters of Oak Creek feel wonderful on your skin. Much of this hike is in the shaded forest, and the slightly higher elevation compared to Sedona can make it a cooler escape when the temperatures really climb.

The West Fork Trail is a wonderful summer excursion with numerous river crossings.

Sterling Pass to Vultee Arch

 34.936633, -111.747192

 5mi, Difficult

 3.5 Hours

 Not Crowded

 ☆☆☆☆☆

 Minimal Coverage

Javelina Cantina

Spring - Fall

Other notable GPS Points:

Vultee Arch Trail Junction:
34.939720, -111.768903

Vultee Arch:
34.941471, -111.768755

Vultee Arch Trailhead (Dry Creek Rd): 34.937220, -111.794447

Below: The arch is as pretty as Devil's Bridge, but less crowded.

Park off the road on N AZ-89A, 4.6 miles north of Midgley Bridge, in the makeshift trailhead lot. It only holds a few cars, which helps keep this trail very quiet.

Hike Sterling Pass 2.6 miles to the Vultee Arch Trail. Sterling Pass is strenuous, as you will immediately begin a steep ascent up the north side of Wilson Mountain before coming to the saddle and descending a series of switchbacks into Sterling Canyon. At the bottom of Sterling Canyon, this trail will dead-end into the Vultee Arch Trail. Follow signage a short distance to the arch. A steep approach up to the arch brings wonderful views of Sterling Canyon.

Another variation on Vultee Arch is to start directly on the Vultee Arch trailhead at the very end of Dry Creek Rd. You will need a high-clearance vehicle for this approach. Don't be fooled by the fairly smooth dirt road as soon as the asphalt ends; this road becomes pretty gnarly later on. Adventurous hikers starting at either trailhead can hike the entire length from Sterling Pass trailhead to Vultee Arch trailhead in just shy of 8 miles round-trip.

A creek crossing followed by a steep ascent up 35 relentless switchbacks along the side of Oak Creek canyon that ends at a fire watchtower makes this quiet hike worthwhile!

AB Young Trail

📍 34.969702, -111.750665

📍 4.8mi, Difficult

🕐 3 Hours

🐾 Not Crowded

👀 ☆☆☆

📊 20% Coverage

🍴 The Table at Junipine

❄️ Spring - Fall

Park at Bootlegger Campground, and then descend straight down to and across Oak Creek. Plenty of stepping stones along the way make for a dry crossing. From here, it's literally all uphill to the end in a series of seemingly never-ending switchbacks to the forest at the top. Note: If you're not immediately heading uphill after crossing the creek, you're on the wrong trail! The AB Young Trail is basically a straight shot across the creek from the parking lot.

At the end of the switchbacks, you'll enter the forest, where the relentless climb eases up to the summit watchtower, pictured above. Though not a technically difficult hike, the elevation gain is significant at over 2,000' in 2.25 miles, earning this trail a difficult rating; this also keeps crowds down and is a nice respite from the Uptown throngs. This hike is best avoided in summer, unless you opt for a very early start!

The view gets better with each and every switchback. You can almost reach out and touch Uptown!

Wilson Mountain

📍 34.885703, -111.741694

📍 11mi, Difficult

🕐 5 Hours

🐾 Not Crowded

👀 ☆☆☆☆☆

📊 50% Coverage

✕ Hideaway House

❄ Spring - Fall

This trail offers a beautiful, varied-terrain hike to the mountain summit, shifting from desert to shrub-land before ending in a full forest at the overlook.

A steep, strenuous hike, Wilson Mountain Trail starts at the Midgley Bridge Picnic area immediately north of the bridge. Follow the signs from the parking lot up to Wilson Mountain Trail, then follow the obvious trail to the top. It's a steep, steady elevation gain right to the top, clocking a whopping 2,800' of elevation gain from trailhead to summit, and as such the landscape changes a few times. The hike begins like a typical Sedona desert hike, then cacti start to disappear and desert shrubs begin to dominate. Eventually, the desertscape changes to shrub-land and small flowering trees dominate, before eventually yielding to the mature forest at the top of the mountain.

This hike is rated as strenuous due to the elevation gain and trail length. For adventurous travelers, make sure to check out the overlook in addition to the true summit, as you gain beautiful views of Sedona and the San Francisco peaks. You can also explore Wilson Canyon Trail, which leaves nearby from the same parking lot as this trail and adds an hour or so to the total hike time, or North Wilson Mountain Trail (which also summits Wilson Mountain, and is a better approach for a hot day). The trailhead for North Wilson Trail can be accessed from the Encinoso Picnic Site, 3.5 miles up AZ-89A from Midgley Bridge.

Above: Varied terrain includes both desert and forest. Below: The view from the summit.

Long and steep, the Hangover Trail is not well used by hikers (it's a double-black mountain bike ride) but is a beautiful trail with fantastic views!

Hangover Loop

📍 34.866479, -111.748485

🗺️ 8.4mi, Difficult

🕐 3.5 Hours

🐾 Not Crowded

🔭 ☆☆☆☆

📶 40% Coverage

🍴 Indian Gardens Cafe

❄️ Fall / Spring

Most will park on Schnebly Hill Rd. at the Munds Wagon Trailhead (if you have a high-clearance vehicle, you can remove the least scenic miles of this hike by parking at Cowpies Trailhead). For the safety of all, we recommend hiking this loop in the opposite direction of mountain bikers (hike clockwise, from Hangover to Cowpies).

This trail starts on Munds Wagon Trail for about two miles, which is the least scenic portion of the trail. Turn left onto the intersection of Hangover, and you'll almost immediately begin a steep ascent that circumnavigates a ledge around the Mitten Ridge formation, pictured below. You'll have a few very steep ascents that nearly approach a Class 2 scramble and certainly gain your legs' attention (and make you question how anyone can ride them on a mountain bike). Just as you want to give up this grueling hike, it'll taper off and give way to easier terrain before arriving at the saddle and high point of the hike. Relax and enjoy the panoramic views of Sedona from the saddle before continuing on. From the saddle, a gentle drop back down less steep ledges gains you access to Cowpies Trail and back to Munds Wagon, completing the 8.4-mile loop. Along the way, just off trail (GPS: 34.876933, -111.726351) the adventurous hiker can seek out a tough-to-find sinkhole, one of Sedona's seven sinkholes and one of the easier ones to access.

Above: Hangover is named for rocks that jut across the trail. Below: Mitten Ridge.

This otherwise easy hike offers added adventures for the avid hiker: caves, vistas, exposure, scrambles, and rappels.

Teacup / Thunder Mtn.

📍 34.874313, -111.796519

📍 2.8mi, Moderate

🕐 1.5 Hours

🌸 Moderately Crowded

🔭 ☆☆☆☆☆

📊 90% Coverage

🍴 Oak Creek Brewery

🗓 Fall - Spring

Park at the Sugarloaf Trailhead on Buena Vista Dr. and hike Teacup to the Thunder Mountain junction. You have a few options for exploration from here. Left onto Thunder Mountain and a very quick right will take you to Keyhole Cave (shown below). To enter the cave and get the photo shown below is a Class 2 to easy Class 3 scramble. Alternatively, continue on Teacup to a quick right on Sugarloaf Loop to the access spur trail to gain the summit of Thunder Mountain.

For a fun little treat for those not afraid of exposure and ledges, follow Teacup to Coffee Pot Rock Trail to the Skidmark Trail. Skidmark is an unofficial trail, but it's very well-worn until the steep end, and you'll follow the clear trail up the side of the rock, gaining a few non-technical ledges on the way. Soon, this will give way to significant exposure (these ledges get steep and narrow and aren't for the faint of heart). You'll be treated to some wonderful views of West Sedona and the base of Coffee Pot Rock. The finish is a very steep Class 2 descent on a rocky trail.

At the end of Skidmark Trail, you'll once again meet up with Teacup Trail and can circle back to the start, or for the very adventurous craving some mileage, continue left on Teacup and take it past Forest Service Rd. 9904 where it meets the Sink Hole spur trail to Devil's Kitchen and Soldier's Pass, then hike Soldier's Pass to the caves and the trail's end (see the hiking description for Soldier's Pass Trail). You can combine everything listed here into one long day's hike past iconic sights, and I promise it'll be a day you'll love (even if your legs hate it)!

Keyhole Cave can be seen from the start of Teacup Trail.

41

Soldier's Pass Trail

📍 34.884232, -111.783693

📏 4.5mi, Moderate

🕐 2.5 Hours + Cave Time

👣 Moderately Crowded

🔭 ☆☆☆☆

📊 50% Coverage

🍴 Mariposa

❄️ All Year

Soldier's Pass has probably more sights crammed into it than any other Sedona area hike: caves, spiritual sights, vistas, sinkholes, and more. The small parking lot even keeps down the crowds.

Begin in the small Soldier's Pass parking lot off of Canyon Shadows Dr. (or take the shuttle from Posse Grounds Park). If the lot is full, avoid street parking. You will be ticketed or towed. You can also park on Eagle Dancer Dr. and hike to the trail via Sugar Loaf Loop, though it adds 2.5 miles round trip (really about 1.8 miles since you'll eliminate the start of the Soldier's Pass hike). Once on the trail, you'll first find Devil's Kitchen sinkhole (Sedona's most active sinkhole, with further collapse predicted), then pass Seven Sacred Pools, a series of naturally carved interconnected pools that serve as a common watering hole for wildlife.

To explore the caves pictured above and below, follow an unmarked turnoff 1.3 miles from the trailhead (GPS 34.896186, -111.786926). This spur trail goes 1/4 mile up a steep ascent to a ridgeline featuring three different caves. Two of the caves can be hiked into, while the third (below) is quite small. The adventurous can follow this ridgeline past the caves to the end and make an exposed Class 2 scramble to Brins Ridge. For most, return back to the main Soldier's Pass Trail and continue to the intersection with Brins Mesa Trail. This ends the formal hike, but those craving more mileage can turn right onto Brins Mesa and head up to Brins Ridge and Brins Mesa Overlook (no scramble needed) for the same beautiful panoramic views.

Right: Devil's Kitchen Sinkhole.
Below: The smallest caves along the spur trail.

Fay Canyon is an easy canyon floor hike, and the hiking time listed here includes a stop at the natural arch, which can be very easy to miss on your first time to the canyon (so use the GPS coordinates). Sitting only a few feet off the main wall, from a distance the arch blends in seamlessly with the rock behind it. As you hike up the main trail, look for a very obvious spur trail at GPS: 34.908248, -111.908248. Cross the dry wash to the right and continues up a short but steep incline to the arch (GPS: 34.908871, -111.862839). It adds about 1/4 mile to the arch and back and is well worth it.

Fay Canyon

📍 34.901849, -111.857353

🧭 2.6mi, Moderate

🕐 2 Hours

👥 Fairly Crowded

🔭 ☆☆☆

📊 20% Coverage

🍴 The Golden Goose

🗓 All Year

Back on the main trail, follow to the official "end of trail" marker, then continue past it and up a sandstone divide in the center of the canyon. Take the ledge either to the left or the right (the left path is recommended). You can hike along the cliff face for a while with views of the backside of Bear Mountain on your left. The trail is easily passable for about 1/4 mile but then begins to fade quickly. The adventurous hiker that followed the left side can loop right around and follow this trail to a scramble that gains an overlook over the canyon. For a great day that makes your legs scream, link up the Bear Mountain, Doe Mountain, and Fay Canyon hikes, back to back to back, for about 5 to 6 grueling hours of hiking. Of these three, Fay Canyon is the easiest.

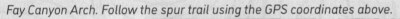

Fay Canyon Arch. Follow the spur trail using the GPS coordinates above.

Bear Mountain

📍 34.893299, -111.865114

📍 5mi, Difficult

🕐 3 Hours

🔴 Moderately Crowded

🔭 ☆☆☆☆☆

📊 40% Coverage

🍴 Pisa Lisa (West Sedona)

❄️ Fall - Spring

A steep, relentless ascent make this one of Sedona's most difficult day hikes, though the views along the entire hike will make you forget how tired you are. This hike is a must-do, every time you visit!

A favorite Sedona hike, Bear Mountain is a relentless ascent up the mountain behind Fay Canyon. Totaling 5 miles round trip, this hike gains over 2,000' of elevation from start to finish and is Sedona's eighth highest summit (but of the top 10, it is one of the most easily accessed). This trail has full-sun exposure, making it less than ideal for summer conditions. A particularly stunning time to hike Bear Mountain is when there is a blanket of snow, or anytime it's cold, as the aggressive elevation gain keeps you warm. At any time of year, bring plenty of water and some snacks.

This hike is difficult but not very technical. There are a few steep rocky sections as well as a few exposed cliff-side areas. All can be passed without difficult scrambling and the hiking is very safe, so don't be deterred if you're on the fence about trying this wonderful hike. Be sure to follow the trail markers (white spray paint on the rocks), as there are a few spur trails that may mislead you, but the main trail is very obvious and well used.

Don't be fooled by the false summit partway up the trail. You'll appear to be approaching the mountain top after a short, steep ascent up a gully around the 1-mile mark, but you'll quickly come to learn that, at this point, you're only about halfway to the summit. Continue to the End of Trail marker and enjoy the view!

The false summit of Bear Mountain is a wonderful spot for picture taking!

Bear Mountain's less-aggressive little sibling, Doe Mountain is a steep ascent up switchbacks but is much shorter than Bear Mountain, ending at a beautiful wide mesa overlooking much of Sedona.

Doe Mountain

- 📍 34.893299, -111.865114
- 📏 2mi, Moderate
- 🕐 1 Hour
- 🐾 Fairly Crowded
- 🔭 ☆☆☆☆☆
- 📶 90% Coverage
- 🍴 Fiesta Mexicana
- ☀️ Fall - Spring

At only two miles round-trip, Doe Mountain is an easy check off your must-do list of West Sedona hikes and is easily combined with Bear Mountain (the two hikes share a parking lot) and/or Fay Canyon. All three can be hiked in a row for the perfect trifecta morning of West Sedona hiking, albeit a long and grueling one. Doe Mountain also intersects the Aerie Trail, making it an ideal stop-off for mountain bikers looking to bag the summit (though Doe Mountain Trail itself is not bikeable, so bring a bike lock).

While Doe Mountain is steep, the hike is quite short, netting it a moderate difficulty rating overall and making it suitable for families with younger children. A mere 400' of elevation gain (20% of Bear Mountain's gain) up non-technical switchbacks brings you to the wide top of this moderately-crowded mesa, where you can wander around the various spur trails freely to find some solitude despite the crowds on the trail. The mesa is massive, and solitude up here is easy to find.

The summit of Doe Mountain is a fantastic spot to enjoy a picnic lunch while taking in the views of Bear Mountain, Wilson Mountain, Chimney Rock, and the Cockscomb; there is no shade on the summit, so plan accordingly. A summer ascent is possible, but this hike is best reserved for the cooler days of fall through spring.

A wide mesa at the top of Doe Mountain is the perfect relaxation spot!

Boynton Canyon

 34.907652, -111.849135

7.3mi, Moderate

4 Hours with Cave Stop

Crowded but Dispersed

☆☆☆☆☆

50% Coverage

Pisa Lisa

Fall - Spring

Boynton Canyon has it all: gorgeous scenery, a vortex, and the well-known Subway Cave. It's no surprise this is one of Sedona's most popular trails.

From the parking lot on Boynton Canyon Rd., follow the trail past the luxury resort. You'll hike a mile or so of open desert with a gradual ascent and beautiful panoramic views before the hike turns into the canyon proper and open desert gives way to forest and slowly narrowing canyon walls, which are equally beautiful and give a striking contrast to the first half of the hike. You'll also pass a few Native American religious sites as well as ruins built into the canyon walls at several places. Observe but don't touch! Be sure to make a stop at the famous Subway Cave, which requires a short Class 2 scramble. Return and continue back up the main trail, which begins to gain elevation more aggressively at this point. Boynton Canyon is a true box canyon, and the hike has a definite end at the back wall of the canyon. The brave can carry on past the sign, but it's not recommended since that area is erosion-prone and route finding and technical hiking ability is required.

Follow the obvious side trail from GPS: 34.927149, -111.860566 to the Subway Cave. The cave is at 34.932301, -111.862814. Later in the day makes for a better photo. Otherwise, the lighting makes you heavily dependent on HDR, as shown below, taken around 11:00am.

A must-do hike if you can handle the crowds, Sedona's largest arch yields some of the most beautiful photographs in Sedona.

Devil's Bridge

📍 34.902834, -111.813866

📍 4mi, Moderate

🕐 1.5 Hours

🐾 Extreme Crowds

🔭 ☆☆☆☆☆

📶 Spotty Coverage

🍴 Sedona Crepes

❄️ All Year

Unfortunately, being Sedona's most popular hike means excessive crowds, especially on weekends. The only time we've seen it fairly quiet was immediately after a snowstorm. That said, it's still a fun hike. You can go a bit past and above the bridge to find a fun and quiet spot to crack a beer and watch everybody queue up for their turn on the bridge. You can also hike under the bridge for a unique perspective.

Devil's Bridge trailhead is along a high-clearance road, and 4-wheel drive vehicles are recommended to access this trailhead. If you're in a passenger car, park at Dry Creek Rd. trailhead (at the end of the asphalt before it turns into a dirt road) and take the ChuckWagon Trail up to Devil's Bridge Trail (adds 4 miles round-trip). An intermediate option is to park at Mescal Trailhead on Long Canyon Rd. and take Mescal to ChuckWagon to Devil's Bridge Trailhead (adds 2.4 miles round-trip compared to parking at Devil's Bridge Trailhead).

Wait-times may exceed 45 minutes to get your photo on the bridge!

Night Hiking

Night hiking in Sedona isn't very popular, but it should be. You'll lose much of the scenery, except on full moon nights, but you'll also lose the crowds and gain an interesting opportunity to see the active animals of the evening. There are javelinas, rabbits, coyote, deer, and more that are most active in the evening hours. Sedona is also an International Dark Sky Community, and building restrictions limit the direction and amount of light from buildings to avoid interfering with stargazing. The result is that the stargazing in Sedona is second to none!

Nighttime Photography

Nighttime photography is quite enjoyable. You'll have the trail pretty much to yourself, so you can set up your gear anywhere you want. Full moonscapes can be fun to shoot, but don't overexpose too much or it will look a bit like daylight. Sedona offers views of the Milky Way band, usually visible in summertime. Photographing this during the cooler nighttime also gives you some time out of the heat. A tripod is mandatory; you'll never be able to handhold the lengths you'll need for good nighttime shots. Setting the camera on a bean bag or pillow on the rock may be a possibility, but you lose the ease-of-use of a good tripod.

Nighttime Safety

On most nights, you'll be the only one on the trail, making it enjoyable, but if you're out alone, stick to areas with cell coverage and make sure someone knows where you'll be and approximately when you'll return. Everything is dialed up a notch at night, meaning you can injure yourself more easily or get into trouble quicker, and the ability of search and rescue to gather quickly and find you is more limited than in the daytime. Use good judgment, and don't extend yourself beyond your abilities.

When night hiking, keep it simple and stick to well-established trails that are mostly flat with limited exposure. Bell Rock Pathway to Big Park Loop, Long Canyon to Mescal Trail, Sugarloaf Loop, Aerie Trail, and Cathedral Rock Loop are all excellent

Long exposure image on a tripod near Bell Rock showing the author's headlamp trail.

options. These areas offer great views for nighttime photos or full moon hikes as well, with the wide panoramic vistas that make night hiking so enjoyable. As a good rule of thumb, carry ample lighting and be redundant. Two lights are better than one, as if one fails, you have a backup. I also like to carry a UV light to see scorpions, as it lights them up like a Christmas tree (see the image below). I don't do this for safety as much as for the photography opportunity. When left undisturbed these creatures are quite harmless, though don't approach too closely. A scorpion sting is no joke; you'll hurt for days, and children may need a hospital.

Shooting the Milky Way is fun, and it's readily visible all summer.

In Sedona, overall the greatest risk to you, is you. Tripping, falling, mis-stepping, and those types of injuries are much more likely at night, though the odds are still quite low if you stick to the easy trails. The risk of injury from animals is very low, provided you don't go chasing after the javelinas. Observe from a distance, and most animals won't care if you're there. Sedona is also a very low-crime city, so the risk from other humans is nearly negligible. Even weather generally seems to cooperate, with most monsoons wrapping up during the daytime hours.

Scorpions react to UV-light and are fun to observe on a warm night. Look, but don't touch!

Technical Hikes / Class 3 & 4 Scrambles

Technical hikes are dangerous! Not for the faint of heart nor those lacking rope skills, technical hikes employ scrambles, rappels, and sketchy exposures to bring you deep into the wilderness. Sedona is a playground full of these types of adventures, but my aim is to expose you to just a small taste of the easier adventures nearby to civilization.

Remember to carry rescue gear, and be prepared to lose cell phone coverage at any time. At a minimum, carry plenty of nutrition, hydration, a harness, helmet, rappel rope & device, and rope ascension system. Most importantly, be trained in the use of all your gear. Sedona is not the place to learn to use it!

Above: Prepare to make many rappels on any technical outing and be well-trained in the use of your gear. Below: Beta for the Courthouse Butte South Bowl technical ascent.

Fun to hike around, but even more fun to ascent, this technical ascent leads to the top of Courthouse Butte. This scramble is classified as a 5.6 rock climb, but there is usually a fixed line at the base of the 5.6 portion that you can ascend. You should use your own judgment as to whether or not you trust the fixed line. You will also want to bring 120' of rope to rappel one section of sketchy Class 4 scrambling, where a misplaced foot on the downclimb will all but guarantee a broken leg or worse. You can make additional rappels down with a longer rope, but the rest can also be scrambled as 3rd Class to shorter low-severity 4th Class.

Approach from the Bell Rock Pathway parking lot, and turn onto Big Park Loop Trail towards the formation. At the tee intersection near the base of the rock, continue on another 1/4 mile to a dry wash. Follow the obvious path that parallels the wash, and scramble up the hill to the base of the rock. An exercise in route finding (see photo left), you'll have to scramble up a few dryfalls and pull a few ledges to get to the Class 4 scramble (20'), then follow up the upper bowl to the right side of a fin. Ascend the fixed rope (note that I cannot guarantee it will be there or be safe), before scrambling another few hundred feet of 3rd Class to the summit. Return the way you came. Rappel the fixed line, walk back down, rappel the 4th Class using your rope on the pitons pictured here (aim over the dryfall where you'll have a fun free-hanging rappel). Then scramble or rappel down the same way you came up. This adventure takes about 3 hours round trip if you know the route, but expect some route finding. You should be a competent and trained scrambler before tackling Courthouse Butte, and carry the gear you need to self-rescue. Cell phone coverage is solid up here.

Courthouse Butte

⚲ 34.791879, -111.761693

⚲ 1.2mi Round-trip

🕐 3 Hours

Not Crowded

👀 ☆☆☆☆☆

📶 100% Coverage

✖ Miley's Cafe

❄ Fall - Spring

A sketchy rappel off two rusty old pitons.

View from the upper bowl looking out over the VOC. 51

Keyhole Cave Rappel

34.874313, -111.796519

3mi Round-trip

5 Hours

Not Crowded

☆☆☆☆

90% Coverage

The Hideaway (Uptown)

Fall - Spring

Located off the Teacup / Thunder Mountain Trail, many hikers will stray from the trail to venture into Keyhole Cave, but few scramble above it and rappel into the cave. It's a cool way to make an entrance!

This outing is an exercise in patience, and parts around the saddle are literally two steps forward, one step back as loose plates of white Coconino sandstone tend to slide all over while you traverse them. Keep plenty of distance between members of your approach party, and minimize rock movement as much as you can. Tread lightly and slowly.

Approach: Park at Teacup Trailhead. Follow Teacup to the intersection with Thunder Mountain. Turn left onto Thunder Mountain, then immediately turn right into the obvious wash. Follow the wash (or the spur trail that parallels it) almost to the base of the cave.

The cave itself will be in sight for most of the hike. As the trail turns steep to the final approach to the cave, stay in the wash past the cave, and follow the wash all the way up to the obvious saddle to the left side of the large rock formation that splits the landscape. Cut up and right at the saddle, then traverse back right along the well-defined ridgeline and over to the cave.

Follow the yellow brick road, the obvious dry wash to the saddle.

The approach starts easy, but quickly turns to a bit of a hot mess as you progress up the canyon wash. Give yourself about 90 minutes to two hours to make the approach, and avoid summer heat. The ridgeline is quite narrow and slow going as well, and there are a few sections of rather short and easy Class 3 scrambling in the wash on the way to the saddle.

Continue along the ridgeline, being careful of the loose, very large sandstone plates and being cognizant of those around you. Minimize damage by treading lightly; this is not a very well-worn path, but a use trail does exist and can be hiked with minimal impact. Try to stay on the rocks as much as possible, and avoid damaging the delicate desert flora. This part of the hike seems never-ending. Just follow the ridge to the top of Keyhole Cave.

The descent comprises three rappels, as follows: R1: 165' off of a tree at the edge of the ledge over the canyon wash, R2: 100' from a bolted anchor, and R3: 160' over the lip of the cave and to the ground. Optionally, R3 can be broken into two rappels, the first into a small hole in the ground that barely fits a human, and the second from a set of anchors inside. This is not for the claustrophobic!

Plan a total round-trip time of 4-5 hours for this excursion. Bring two 60m ropes and a helmet, as there is a lot of loose rock on this trail and in the canyon proper.

The cave is also quite busy with hikers, many unfamiliar with what yelling "rope" means, so do your best to lower your rope slowly for the final rappel into or over the cave (or bag it).

Rock Climbing

Icon Guide:
- Wall GPS
- ⏄ Climb Height
- ⌢ YDS Difficulty
- 🏆 Climb Rating
- 📶 Cell Coverage
- ⚔ # Climbs or Pitches

Note: Climbing is dangerous and requires training. This is not a comprehensive climbing guide. Climb at your own risk, as Sedona is chossy and sandbagged!

The author rappelling off The Mace.

A classic 5-pitch line, the Original Route up The Mace is one of Sedona's most fun lines and one of the earliest established routes, ascending the popular hiking destination Cathedral Rock. Sedona mainly has old-school trad climbing, and the route will feel sandbagged by modern standards. But you'll get a nice boost of adrenaline from the cheers from nearby hikers, and as you summit the tower, you'll be treated to 360° views of the Village of Oak Creek.

This route has a little bit of everything: fist cracks, finger cracks, offwidth (enough to keep it interesting, but for you offwidth haters, there's only 20' or so), plus face climbing and even a small amount of slab. The denouement is a very committing lean across a tower onto the summit tower to a bolt, followed by a leaning traverse to a flake, and a step across to a 5.8 slab finish. This part is quite heady (you'll be looking down at a 200' drop over the 1-meter gap between towers), and newer leaders may want to use a cheater draw to clip before making the move. Rappel the summit to the main tower. Two more rappels with a single 70m rope get you to the ground.

The Mace - Original

📍 34.818462, -111.790855

⚖ Height: 300'

🪝 Rating: 5.9+

🏆 ☆☆☆☆☆

📊 100% Coverage

🧗 Trad, 5 Pitches

The start of Pitch 3 is a very exposed face traverse, but on good holds.

Left: The start of the first pitch. Approach the tower by starting on Cathedral Rock trail. Towards the end of the hike, follow the climber's trail to the base of the easternmost (left) tower (see beta image below).

Beta for The Mace - Original route.

The Planetarium

📍 34.834356, -111.768450

📐 Height: 80'

🔄 Rating: 5.10a - 5.12d

🏆 ☆☆☆

🔋 100% Coverage

🧗 10 Sport, 2 Trad

Sedona single-pitch sport at its finest, The Planetarium features two walls connected by a small cave with a short 10-minute approach. It's no surprise this area is so popular. A variety of overhanging technical moves, balancy climbing, slab, and roof, climbing here is technical, difficult, and fun.

Approach: Park at Mystic Trailhead (Chapel Rd). Follow the trail a few hundred yards to an obvious climber's trail up to The Planetarium, the cave shown below is the obvious landmark to sight to. The below is not a complete list of the sport lines but are some of my favorites.

Infinite Improbability Drive
5.11a

Muppets In Space
5.10d

The Rear wall of the Planetarium (top left) is accessed through a short cave (top right). Below: Beta shot of the front wall of the Planetarium, visible from the Mystic Trailhead.

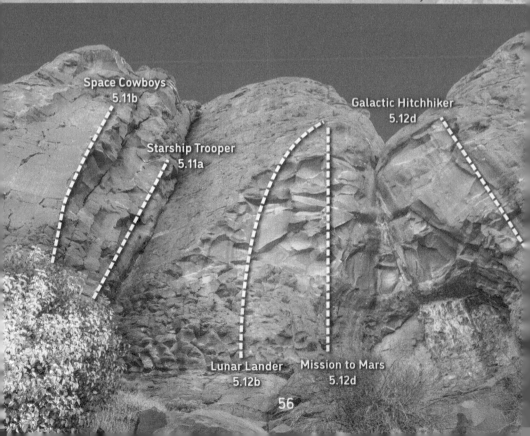

Space Cowboys
5.11b

Starship Trooper
5.11a

Galactic Hitchhiker
5.12d

Lunar Lander
5.12b

Mission to Mars
5.12d

A fun excursion up Gibraltar Rock in the VOC, this moderate climb follows fairly solid rock (at least by Sedona standards) and is bound to become a classic.

Approach: Park at Little Horse, hike Bell Rock Pathway to Little Horse to Llama. At 0.5 miles down Llama, turn left into a small wash (GPS: 34.820833, -111.761232). Note, on Google Map there is a false pin named "Upper Wash Approach." Don't be misled, and follow the GPS coordinates above. From here, follow another 0.3 steep miles to the start of the climb.

Sedona Scenic Cruise

📍 34.818462, -111.754292

△↕ Height: 700'

⌒ Rating: 5.9

🏆 ☆☆☆☆☆

📊 100% Coverage

🤸 Trad, 5 Pitches

Start on the obvious flake, and work your way up 5 pitches of solid climbing. Note, pitch 2 begins behind the tree, not from the pitch 1 anchors. Bring up your second from the anchors, then move the belay to behind the tree.

This route has bolted belay stations without chains, and bolted rappel stations with chains. Don't be misled off-route chasing stations with chains, as you'll use these only for the descent, which requires two-rope rappels (a 70m will NOT get you down with one rope).

At the end of the fifth pitch, a short scramble is required to gain the true summit. Finish it off, then enjoy panoramic views to Courthouse Butte and Twin Buttes.

Road Biking

Although not as well known for road biking as mountain biking, Sedona is well laid-out and features bike lanes in most areas connecting the Village of Oak Creek, Uptown, and West Sedona, making it very well suited for road bikers. Use caution, as many drivers are easily distracted by the beautiful scenery, drive 20 mph in excess of the posted 35 mph speed limit, or both. A rear flasher is highly recommended.

Road biking in Sedona is a wonderful means of transportation. Sedona has a traffic problem; often times you can bike from the VOC to Uptown in about the same time as you can drive it, plus you're always guaranteed parking.

My favorite road bike route is a 39-mile loop through Cornville, West Sedona, Uptown, and the VOC. Riding the route clockwise is recommended, as you gain the most fun descents in this direction.

As you might expect, Sedona is quite hilly. 13% grades for short stretches are not uncommon, and prolonged ascents or descents of 6-8% are quite common, with a few lasting over a mile. This loop has a total ascent / descent of 2,300' in 39 miles and can be ridden in anywhere from 2 to 3 hours by typical riders.

Along the way, you'll have access to most of Sedona's trails. In Cornville, you'll have access to some of the Sedona area's best wineries, along the stretch of Page Springs Rd., so I encourage you to stop there for a restful lunch at your halfway point, grab a glass of wine, and ponder how people can grow grapes in the desert!

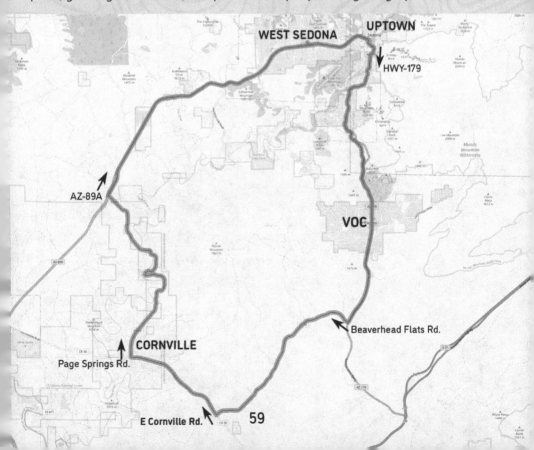

Mountain Biking - Village of Oak Creek Area

The Village of Oak Creek (VOC) has some of Sedona's finest mountain biking, as well as the largest range of rides from easy to extreme, from the beginner's Bell Rock Pathway to the adrenaline junkie's HiLine and High on the Hog double black diamond trails, and everything in between from fast and flowy to technical and tricky. For good measure, there's even a solid jump trail (Pigtail). In a long weekend of mountain biking, you could easily spend the entirety in the VOC and not get bored!

Unlike hiking, where most people tend to get on one trail and see it through to completion, Sedona mountain bikers will connect multiple trails in a single session. Therefore, I'll discuss mountain biking in all Sedona regions in terms of the multiple trails that make up a ride, and discuss options to add or subtract difficulty by choosing your route, rather than focusing on a single trail at a time.

What makes Sedona biking great is that you can bike almost anywhere, wilderness aside. This means most hiking trails are bike-friendly (and horse friendly), and with that comes a need for proper etiquette. Remember, as a biker you yield to everyone - hikers and horses. Amongst other bikers, when it's narrow, always yield to the uphill rider. You'll find in Sedona most hikers are very accepting of and friendly towards bikers. When you get to the epic descents, you may even get an audience!

Bell Rock Pathway & Big Park Loop Trails

The best area for beginners, these fun beginner to intermediate trails offer the option to connect to more advanced riding in the Hog Trails or Yavapai Vista.

Park at the Bell Rock Trailhead lot on the east of 179. Bell Rock Pathway is a beginner and child-friendly trail that is mostly flat and passes the iconic Bell Rock formation and continues on all the way up to the difficult Little Horse trailhead. The closer you get to Little Horse, the hillier this trail gets, but it always remains non-technical and beginner friendly. The start of this trail is always packed full of hikers and can be an exercise in patience (there is a singletrack bypass about 1/2 mile in, but this is technical). When ridden from south to north, this trail is more uphill than down and makes a great warm-up ride for advanced riders connecting to nearby trails. At the south end of this trail is the connector to Big Park Loop, another easy, family-friendly trail with the exception of a few moderately technical dry wash crossings that can easily be walked. Big Park Loop is very wide and flowy and another great beginner or warm-up spot, and can be shortened via Middle Trail, which bisects Big Park Loop into two smaller loops.

The more advanced biker will use Bell Rock Pathway as a warm up, or skip it by parking at Courthouse Vista. If the latter, a short jaunt on Bell Rock Pathway takes you to either the west side of Highway 179 via Templeton to ride the more difficult Yavapai Vista area trails, or to Little Horse and the Hog trails (you can also approach Little Horse from the Llama Trail, which is a step up from Bell Rock Pathway in excitement and difficulty). If connecting on, I personally, I favor the Hog trails over most of the Yavapai Vista trails; they're just more interesting.

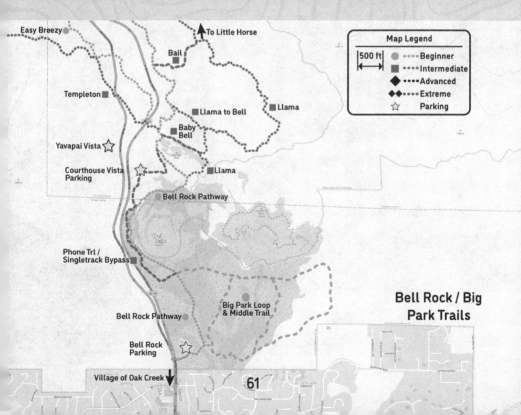

Llama is a great trail to take to approach Little Horse and the Hog trails, and if you're a more advanced rider, you'll prefer it over Bell Rock Pathway. It offers a few fun descents and climbs in and out of small washes, and has a few rock gardens to pass, but nothing terribly technical. For a full day of great riding, take Llama to Little Horse to the end, then connect into the Hog trails, which opens you to several blue, black, and double black options, with an easy green return. You're committed to the mileage with this loop, as there is no shortcut back from the Hog trails to the start other than to ride it out. If you can hang with it, though, you're in for a treat. Bring plenty of water, as there is nowhere to fill up on your ride and there is no easy-off to a convenience store or other refill station on this loop.

Another option is to cross Hwy 179 on Templeton Trail, which opens you up to the Yavapai Vista trails (including the double-black HiLine Trail). If you do these trails, you'll want to ride Templeton south-to-north until you hit your desired connector. See the *Yavapai Vista Area Trails* section for more details about these trails.

Finally, if you're parked at the southernmost lot, Bell Rock parking, be sure to ride the singletrack bypass you'll see, which starts nearby the Courthouse Vista parking area and bypasses the throngs of hikers. In addition to being a fun, technical downhill ride, it will save you the headache of passing hikers at speed. It rides best north-to-south.

Little Horse Trail, at Chicken Point.

Yavapai Vista Area Trails

Park at the Yavapai Vista parking lot, accessible only from 179-Southbound, or Bell Rock or Courthouse Vista (if the latter two, take Bell Rock Pathway to Templeton to the west side of 179).

If you're crunched for time, you can pack a ton of variety into a short amount of time in this region. Many riders come exclusively for the HiLine, the super-steep humbling double black trail. A caution on the HiLine: make sure you're up to this challenge. It's one-way, so once you start, you can't bail until the halfway point. The first half of the trail is also relatively easy (exposed but not super technical), so it's easy to gain a false sense of security. From the halfway point, this trail is steep and technical. You can test-ride the first half and see how it goes. If it's feeling easy, then stick with it, but be ready for it to turn steep and gnarly. If the first half is too much, bail onto the Transept Trail before the extremely technical and steep sections begin.

If you're not here for the HiLine, you're still in for a treat. Slim Shady and Templeton are two very popular trails. It is best to park at Bell Rock Pathway, ride Bell Rock under the highway to Templeton, then Templeton up to Cathedral Rock to the junction of Easy Breezy. Though you can continue on Templeton and connect into Baldwin to gain creek access, the riding past the Cathedral Rock Trail junction isn't as nice (though on a hot day, Templeton turns shady past this junction).

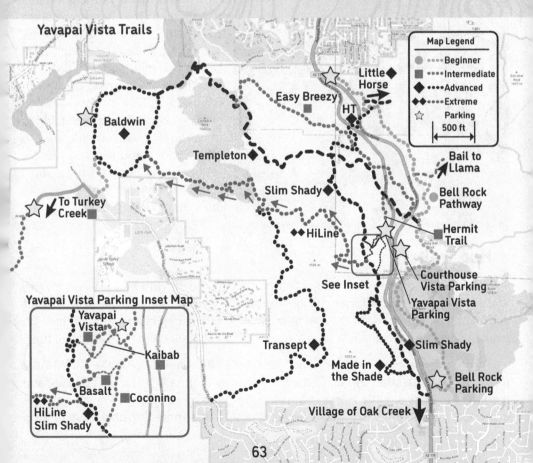

63

From Templeton just before the Cathedral Rock junction, head down Easy Breezy to the short HT connector, up to Slim Shady, then ride Slim Shady from north to south (this is the more fun direction, and riding from south to north is a slugfest that omits the fun and twisty natural berms). Slim Shady will end you right across Hwy 179 from the Bell Rock Pathway parking lot.

Options to expand include looping on Made in the Shade (also best ridden north to south, and more technical than the Slim Shady Trail). This trail is very rocky, however, and most prefer Slim Shady, which is really the classic moderate for the area (with HiLine being the classic extreme).

To connect into Little Horse and the Hog trails, take the HT Trail from the north end of this system to Bell Rock Pathway and up to Little Horse. For riders with good endurance, linking the two systems makes for a great day of riding.

If you check the inset map on the previous page, you'll see several short trails (Kaibab, Yavapai Vista, and Basalt). These are each a quarter mile or so in length, and it doesn't matter which one you take, as they're all about the same length and difficulty and only serve to connect you to the better trails above.

One final note: there is a newly installed maintenance center at the trailhead,

complete with most of the tools you'd need for any minor repairs to your bike. This is a great place to remember if you need a quick maintenance check and don't want to pay the bike shop to do it for you. These are popping up all over Sedona, and I love it! Last year, I had a major save at Fay Canyon parking lot when I drove all the way to West Sedona and realized I forgot to tighten my pedals. I hope you'll never need these, but it's nice to know they exist if you do.

Hog Trails

Some of Sedona's finest riding, the Hog trails combine with Little Horse, Mystic, and a short excursion on the road to form one of the best loops in all of Sedona, without sucking up an entire day. You can ride much of this loop in just a few hours, then go over and explore Yavapai Vista area trails to complete a full-day of two wheeled fun.

My preferred approach to the Hog Trails is via Little Horse. Park in the Little Horse parking lot, take a short trip on Bell Rock Pathway to the Little Horse trailhead, and then the fun begins. Little Horse is a moderate climb up to Chicken Point where the trail ends and becomes Broken Arrow. Broken Arrow is more downhill than up from here, and moderately technical and fun for the intermediate rider. For the advanced rider, Broken Arrow splits off to the two double-blacks High on the Hog and Hog Heaven. If you try the first double-black and it's too much for you, you can bail on Twin Buttes. Otherwise continue on through to the super-fast Pigtail jumpline then follow Mystic and the on-road connector back to Chapel Trail. More intermediate-level riders should skip the double-blacks and stay on Broken Arrow, connecting to Hog Wash and ending on Mystic to the on-road connector and looping back Chapel to Little Horse and back to the car (or down Bell Rock Pathway and over to the Yavapai Vista area).

If you've parked at Broken Arrow parking, you'll have a few options. You can start directly on Broken Arrow up to High on the Hog, or you can climb Hog Wash to the end and either session Pigtail (the jump trail) or connect down to Mystic. I recommend parking at Little Horse. Not only is parking easier to find, but it's a more fun way to ride this trail system. In fact, you can even park at Courthouse Butte and take Llama to Little Horse to the Hog Trails, which gains you a nice warm-up and a fun, fast downhill back to your car at the end.

One note if you're connecting from the On-Road Connector to Chapel Trail: The Chapel Trail marker is hard to see, as it's short and usually blocked by cars. On your final ascent to the base of the church, look for angled parking on the right-hand side of the road. Behind these cars is the trailhead marker, tucked lower to the ground.

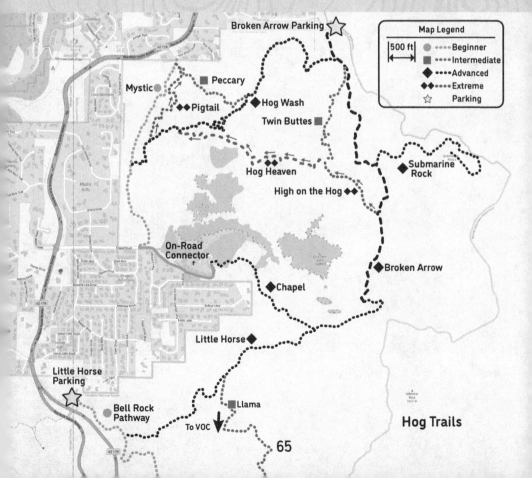

Mountain Biking - Uptown Area

Only one small trail system in Uptown is listed here: the Hangover Loop (some lump the Hog trails with Uptown, but the Hog trails connect more readily to the other VOC trail systems so we list them there).

Despite there being only one loop, it's a darn good one. The infamously known Hangover Trail is best reserved for extreme, technically-adept mountain bikers only. Large drop-offs, narrow cliff-side ledges, and some of the steepest riding in Sedona is found on the Hangover Trail!

Hangover Loop

If you're coming Uptown to bike, it's probably to ride the Hangover Trail. This is Sedona's gnarliest double black and about the most fun you can have on two wheels here. Hangover is very advanced: steep, narrow, and exposed. It also features numerous 3'-4' drop-offs and numerous other technical sections. If this is your jam, saddle up, hang on, and let 'er rip!

If you're not up to the challenge of the double-black Hangover, avoid the Uptown area, as there is better and more ample riding to be had elsewhere in Sedona. For short and technical rides, head to the VOC and for longer and more flowy trails, head to West Sedona. But if you can handle the Hangover Trail, you're in for a treat!

If you have a high-clearance vehicle, park on Schnebly Hill Rd. at the trailhead for Cowpies (GPS: 34.872070, -111.712974), which takes you to the Hangover. You'll save considerable mileage parking here, but if you don't have a high-clearance vehicle, park at Munds Wagon trailhead and follow that trail past the end of Hangover to the start of Cow Pies (Hangover is one-way, downhill trail).

Hang on, enjoy the ride, and treat yourself to a nice cold beer at the end of this hangover. Trust me, you've earned it!

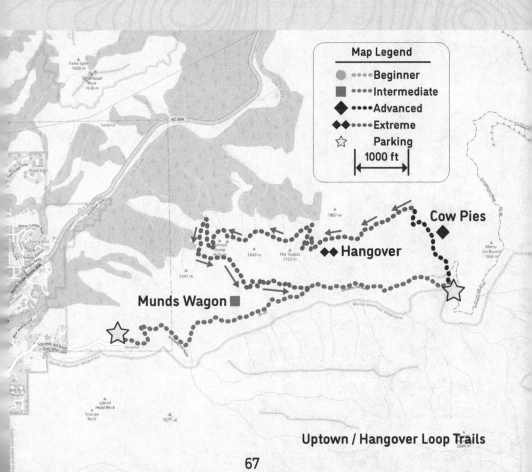

Uptown / Hangover Loop Trails

Mountain Biking - West Sedona

The largest concentration of trails in the Sedona area and the most fun trails for moderate-level flowy riding are found in West Sedona. You'll find a few green (beginner) trails here and tons of blues (intermediate) and blacks (advanced) but no double-blacks here. These trails ride quick and flowy, and you can easily rake up the miles before you know it. 30+ mile days can fly right by!

The regions shown here can generally be connected together, but within each region there is well more than a day's worth of riding, so you won't really need to link up the areas unless you want to. Parking in West Sedona is ample, with numerous lots and roadside parking. If you're in a mood to crush out some miles, West Sedona should be your go-to.

If you're not sure where to start, check out the Dry Creek area and take Mescal Trail to Canyon of Fools (two fantastic trails in the area, though Canyon of Fools can get pretty wrecked in the monsoon season). Mescal Trail offers beautiful non-technical riding with lots of slickrock and is a fun example of Sedona riding at its finest without being super technical. Ample opportunities also exist from here to link up to other trails (both easier and harder) to really pack on some miles. If you're pressed for time, Adobe Jack has some shorter trails with good climbs to help you get your lungs open quickly, and it is often less crowded than other areas.

Adobe Jack Area

A fun series of hilly trails, this area is more fun to ride from north to south (downhill), but you'll have to climb up to the top somehow. I recommend the Adobe Jack proper trail to climb, as it's less technical (blue-rated). Cut back down the hill on any trail or sequence of trails including Grand Central, Powerline Plunge, or Javelina. For advanced riders, extend your mileage by cutting across Teacup to Thunder Mountain and take a loop around Lower Chimney Rock.

If you're looking to pack on some easier miles, climb Jordan to Jim Thompson, then head 5 miles one-way on Jim Thompson. Horse Alert: this is a popular equestrian trail, so remember to yield to horseback riders. There is no good option other than to retrace your path back unless you've arranged a car shuttle, as the ending of Jim Thompson is a little ways up AZ-89A by the Midgley Bridge and it's a long route back via AZ-89A if you don't backtrack.

As far as individual trails in the core Adobe Jack region, you really can't go wrong. They're all fairly hilly, moderately technical (but passable by most newer riders), and very short, meaning you can hit them all, back to back. This lets you session them out with minimal time commitment; a few hours in the Adobe Jack area will get your lungs open, heart pumping, and have you feeling great! If you're searching for a quick but intense workout, Adobe Jack is a wonderful place to ride.

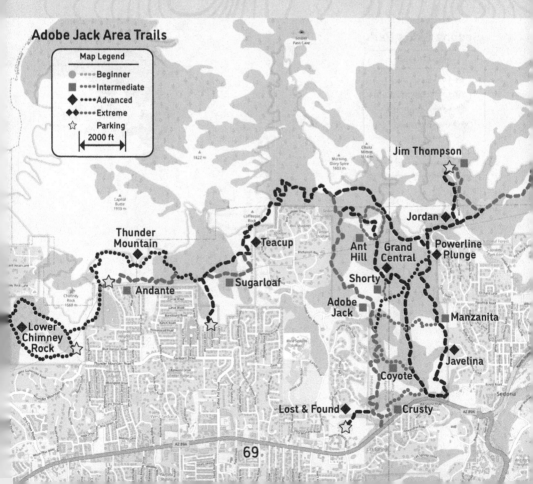

Adobe Jack Area Trails

Map Legend
- Beginner
- Intermediate
- Advanced
- Extreme
- Parking
- 2000 ft

Sedona Bike Skills Park

If you ride like me, a little refresher never hurts! This bike park is a great warm up before the main adventure, or if you're in town longer, a great controlled environment to hone your bike handling skills. Readily accessible just off the main drag of AZ-89A on Posse Grounds Rd., there's just enough here if you're pressed for time but want to squeeze in some training. Expertly crafted, you'll be greeted with a variety of one-way trails (black and blue on the map below) and a few return trails (green on the map below). Features include a pump track, dual slalom run, a few flow trails, a drops course, and a few low-key return trails to the top.

One of the best features of the bike park is that it offers specific training for the riding experience in Sedona. If you're new to biking and want to test yourself on the flow trails before hitting the real trails, this is a great way to evaluate your skills. Similarly, if you're contemplating the double-blacks in town, this can be a good way to test your readiness for those epic adventures.

If you've ever wondered how the people that ride the drops and steeps of the Hangover or crush the twisty descents of the HiLine do it, it's time in the saddle at skills courses like these! Proper fundamentals in controlled settings set you up for success on the trail!

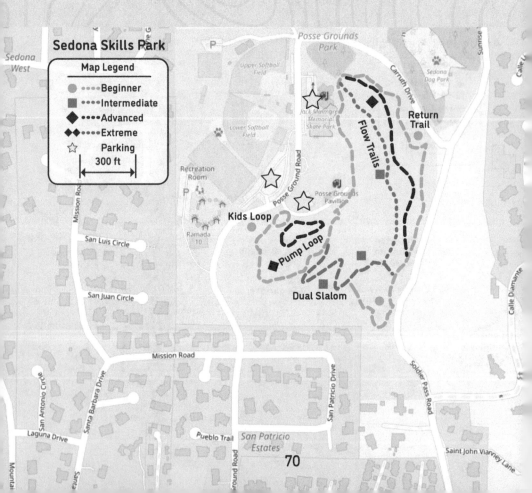

South of AZ-89A

A well-interconnected trail system with a variety of trailheads, there is no "best" way to ride these trails. Park wherever is most convenient based on where you're coming from, and start pedaling! Some trails, like Schuerman Mountain and Scorpion, are best ridden north to south to take advantage of the downhills, but without a car shuttle, you'll end up riding back up (or following the road up) anyways.

Airport Loop is a good but rocky trail with some areas of cliff-side exposure steep enough to keep you alert and concentrating, but not enough to make it as scary as the Hangover, and is a good venture before tackling the double-blacks.

In between Schuerman Mountain and the 3-mile Airport Loop is a lot of great quality, moderate-level riding, all well interconnected to make it easy to customize the length of your ride as well as the difficulty. Bandit is a 1/2-mile moderate but fast downhill to Carroll Canyon, while Brewer is often used as a connector to more parking, but is also a fun downhill from Airport Loop, not quite a mile long and moderately steep with many good dropoffs.

If riding after a rainy day, Skywalker is one of the go-to's in the area, as it's often dry within a few hours of a major monsoon rainfall (it also offers attention-getting climbs to the high-point of this region, yielding spectacular views and tired legs).

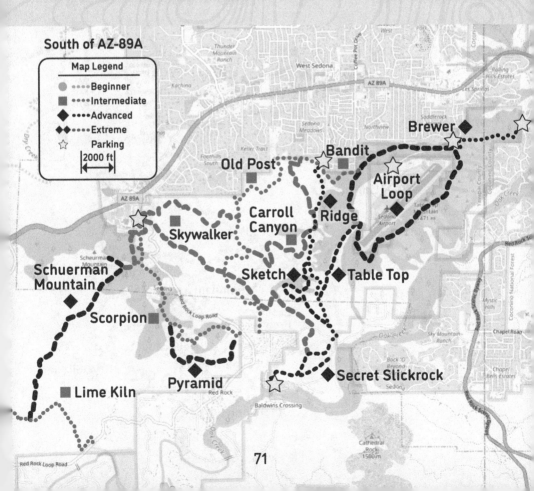

Cultural Park Area Trails

Hilly moderate routes with a smattering of short technical downhills, Ledge-n-Airy and Last Frontier are the fun go-to's in this area. These are best ridden south to north, starting on Outer Limits from the Girdner trailhead and proceeding downhill. In fact, ledges, drops, and generally steep riding may make these sections impassable on an uphill climb, so plan your return route accordingly. It's most common to simply return via Girdner, which is steep but not technical.

The upper sections of this trail system ride downhill from north to south, and if starting by the parking lot near Two Fence Trail, you'll be mostly flat-to-descending much of the way towards the Girdner trailhead, with the final 30% or so being steep uphill.

If you're looking for a moderate adventure, ride the loop consisting of Outer Limits and Girdner. This will be at a minimum a 10-mile adventure, and depending on what trail you choose to link Girdner to Outer Limits, you can easily extend it from here. Cockscomb to Rupp will be the shortest linkup, while the longest will include linking Cockscomb to the Dry Creek Rd. trails and circling a meandering lap of this region before returning to the trailhead. Riding up to 30 miles is easy to achieve. This linkup lets you gain some serious mileage with some wonderful red rock views everywhere but without anything too techy or demanding that an intermediate rider can't handle.

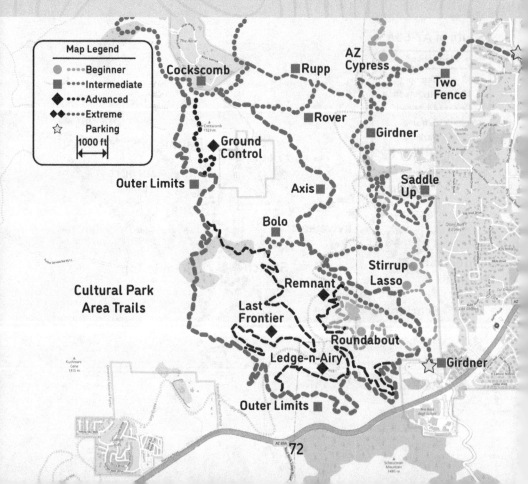

Dry Creek Road Trails

Long moderates reign supreme here; Dry Creek Rd. features the best collection of blue-rated rides in Sedona, all connected by short connector trails or loops and tons of parking areas with easy linkups to the Cultural Park trails. You can't beat this location for a full-day of low-tech, high-mileage riding.

For the absolute beginner staying in West Sedona, Long Canyon provides a great introduction to mountain biking and is about as easy as it gets in Sedona, probably even easier than Bell Rock Pathway in the VOC. It's smooth, well-graded hardpack with minimal elevation gain, though it's quite short.

A preferred moderate route is to start at the Mescal trailhead, climb around Mescal Mountain to Deadman's Pass, descend Long Canyon, loop ChuckWagon, and then repeat the start of Mescal. On this second lap, drop into Canyon of Fools, a fun, fast downhill that ends through a small slot canyon with a jumpline (when it's not washed out from monsoons). If desired, lap this portion by returning on Yucca.

From the end of Canyon of Fools, let your legs be your guide. You can power out more mileage following Dawa to Cockscomb to Aerie, looping the southern part of this trail system. Or follow Axis or Girdner to connect into the Cultural Park Area trails for even more riding on some of Sedona's newer trails. You'll gain some sweet downhills into the Cultural Park system, so we aware of the steep ascent to return!

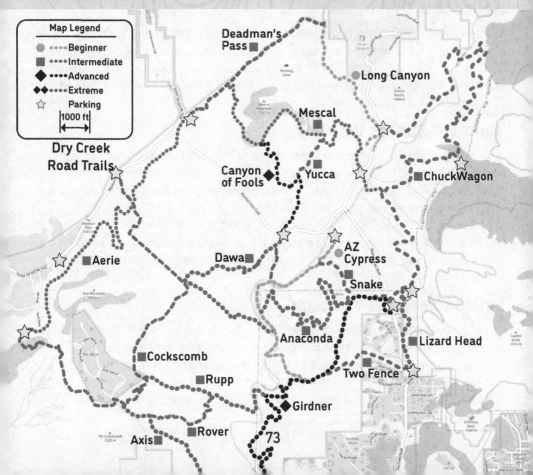

Map Legend
- Beginner
- Intermediate
- Advanced
- Extreme
- Parking

1000 ft

Dry Creek Road Trails

Deadman's Pass

Long Canyon

Mescal

Canyon of Fools

Yucca

ChuckWagon

Aerie

Dawa

AZ Cypress

Snake

Anaconda

Lizard Head

Cockscomb

Rupp

Two Fence

Girdner

Rover

Axis

73

Family Friendly Activities

Tlaquepaque Arts / Crafts Village

Say it like a local: tuh-la-keh-pah-keh. As fun to shop as it is to say, the Tlaquepaque shopping village features easy parking and numerous art stores where local artists display their art on a wide variety of mediums including canvas, photography, sculptures, and more. In addition, numerous restaurants and eateries can be found here, including Oak Creek Brewery, a coffee shop, and an ice cream shop. What more do you need? (tlaq.com)

Hot Air Balloon Rides

These can be a truly romantic (or the total opposite, a very child-friendly) way to explore Sedona from a unique perspective. Check out Red Rock Balloons (RedRockBalloons.com) or Northern Lights Balloon Expeditions (NorthernLightsBalloons.com), the only two permitted companies in Sedona. Or, if you're a balloon aficionado, plan your trip around the world's largest hot air balloon festival, a five-hour drive away in Albuquerque, New Mexico, which usually runs in October.

Helicopter Tours

Faster and noisier than a hot air balloon and not subject to the whims of the wind, a helicopter tour is just the ticket for a higher speed, adrenaline-packed adventure around the skies of Sedona. Get bird's eye views of the best rock formations in town. Check out Guidance Air (GuidanceAir.com), Apex Air (FlyApexAir.com), or Sedona Air Tours (SedonaAirTVours.com).

Sunrise / Sunset Viewing

If balloon rides or helicopters aren't your thing, but you still want to be near the airport, one of the best sunrise and sunset viewing spots in Sedona is from Airport Mesa overlook. Just a short hike (5 minutes or less) up mildly steep terrain yields a massive mesa where you can relax and take in panoramic views. This is a very popular spot for watching the sunset, so don't expect solitude, but do expect a beautiful experience. Because the approach is short, you can also pack a bit heavy; this is a great spot to haul a picnic, comfy chair, or any other glamping accessories you choose!

Sedona Heritage Museum

Listed on the National Register of Historic Places, the Sedona Heritage Museum is a great place to observe and appreciate the history of Sedona. Open daily 11:00 to 3:00 and costing only $7 (children under 13 free), this is one of the most affordable things you can do on your trip to Sedona. If you're eloping to Sedona, the heritage museum also makes a great wedding venue. (SedonaMuseum.org)

Jeep / Driving Tours

Whether you want a laid-back, tarmac-smooth ride or a rugged, brain-rattling 4x4 off-road adventure, Sedona has you covered. Options include Pink Jeep Tours (PinkAdventureTours.com), Scenic Sedona Tours (ScenicSedonaTours.com), A Day in the West Tours (ADayInTheWest.com), Sedona Offroad Adventures (SedonaOffroadAdventure.com), and Sedona Trolley (SedonaTrolley.com). Each offers multiple tour options.

4x4 / UTV Rentals

Don't like being chauffeured around? Rent your own dune buggy or ATV / UTV and take the wheel yourself at any of the numerous ATV trails in and around Sedona. Rent at Sedona ATV Rentals (ATVSedona.com), Outback ATV (OutbackATV.com), or Sedona Off-Road Center (SedonaOffRoadCenter.com). Great trails include Schnebly Hill OHV Trails, Broken Arrow, Diamondback Gulch, Cliffhanger, or Dry Creek.

Sedona Film Festival

If you're looking for a fun silver screen experience, the Sedona International Film Festival is a must-do event. Hosted every February and lasting just over a week, this film festival screens well over 100 movies, ranging anywhere from student films, shorts, documentaries, and more, in three theaters. Tickets are available to the public, and if you can't make it during the actual film festival, the theaters routinely replay the best of the best throughout the year. Check out their website to see what's screening when you're in town (SedonaFilmFestival.com). If you're used to a large, crowded theater at home, you're in for a nice intimate treat at the Mary D. Fisher or Alice Gill-Sheldon Theatres, the latter of which is pictured below.

Bearizona Wildlife Park

It's like Arizona, but with more bears (and elk, foxes, wolves, deer, bison, and more). Located in Williams, Arizona on historic Route 66, Bearizona is an 80-minute drive from Sedona and well worth it. This drive-through wildlife park and can easily be combined with a visit to the Grand Canyon. Three hours lets you see much of the park before continuing on to the canyon. Keep in mind that the animals are generally more active earlier in the day, so plan accordingly and arrive early. The more natural setting means you'll never know which animals will greet you! (Bearizona.com)

Out of Africa Wildlife Park

Located in nearby Camp Verde, Arizona (30 minutes from VOC), this zoo features animals you certainly won't see on the Sedona trails, including giraffes, tigers, zebras, and more. Hours vary seasonally, so check them out online. (OutOfAfricaPark.com)

Blazin' M Ranch

Not quite in Sedona (about 30 minutes away in nearby Cottonwood, Arizona), the Blazin' M Ranch is a western-themed frontier town complete with saloon, shooting range, and something you won't find hiking West Sedona's ChuckWagon Trail: an authentic chuckwagon dinner! (BlazinM.com)

Snowbowl (Skiing)

Visiting in winter? Arizona is one of the few states where you can hike in warm weather on the same day you gear up to ski. Snowbowl isn't in Sedona; it's about an hour north in Flagstaff, located on the west side of Mount Humphrey (Arizona's tallest mountain). The ski resort boasts 55 runs, each up to 2 miles long in over 2,800' of skiable elevation and nearly 800 acres of terrain. If that's not enough ski-related statistics for you, the 260" of snow per year should be! Visiting in summer? Humphrey's Peak Trail starts at Snowbowl (see the *Outside Sedona* section). (www.Snowbowl.ski)

Verde Canyon Railroad

All aboard! Passengers on the Verde Canyon Railroad enjoy living-room-style seating, appetizers, and a complimentary champagne toast, making this train ride a lavish way to see a rugged and untouched part of Arizona. Perfect for your rest day from hiking, and located just 30 minutes from Sedona, this railroad features complimentary open-air gondolas interspersed throughout the train's quarter-mile length. (VerdeCanyonRR.com)

Sedona UFO Tours

No travel guide to Sedona would be complete without mentioning Sedona UFO Tours. Because, you know, Sedona. Seriously, this tour is the best way to learn about the stars, satellites, and other objects of lesser-known origin that ominously loom above us. Your tour guide will supply night vision goggles, so all you need to bring is an open mind and a willingness to learn about the night sky! Sedona UFO Tours also provides vortex, meditation, and general sightseeing tours. (SedonaUFOtours.com)

Chapel of the Holy Cross

It's not the only church in Sedona, but Chapel of the Holy Cross' unique architecture, with seamless integration into the surrounding red rock landscape certainly gains it more attention than the others, making it a must-see on your list. Built into the side of Twin Butte, expect a short but steep walk up to the chapel. You can also link up to several hiking trails nearby (Little Horse, Mystic, and Chapel). You can tour this church from 9:00am to 5:00pm, 363 days per year. Ironically, it's closed Christmas and Easter. (ChapeOfTheHolyCross.com)

Wineries & Breweries

I had a coworker who would routinely mispronounce Sedona as "Sonoma." Perhaps this was a subconscious statement about the wineries in the Sedona region rivaling those of California. For a desert community, there sure are a lot of fantastic vineyards to be found in the area. Below is a curated list of favorites.

If driving yourself to a winery doesn't sound prudent, there's also a list of tour companies here that will handle the driving for you, letting you focus your efforts on the more important things, like drinking Arizona-made wine!

Sedona Area

Winery 1912

Winery 1912 produces wines in the Dragoon Mountains in Cochise County, Arizona (just southeast of Tucson) and offers tastings in its Uptown Sedona tasting room, located at 320 N AZ-89A. (Winery1912.com)

Vino Zona

Vino Zona is not a vineyard or winery, but rather a tasting room where you can taste a variety of Arizona wines, all hand-picked by the experts of Vino Zona. A second Vino Zona location can be found in nearby Jerome, Arizona. (VinoZona.com)

Secret Garden Cafe at Tlaquepaque

While not a winery, this cafe has a specialty wine bar and is also conveniently located in the heart of Sedona in Tlaquepaque Village. Also on tap are many Arizona beers! (SedonaSecretGardenCafe.com)

Cornville

When people talk about visiting the Sedona vineyards, it's usually the ones in nearby Cornville they're talking about, as most of the wineries elsewhere around Sedona do not grow grapes on site. These Cornville wineries are the closest to West Sedona and just a few minutes off AZ-89A.

Page Springs Cellars

A beautiful vineyard, Page Springs Cellars features tours of the winery, strolls through the vineyard, a tasting room, and even various activities like vineyard yoga. (PageSpringsCellars.com)

Oak Creek Vineyards

Featuring a pet-friendly patio, an indoor tasting room, and a variety of wines from sweet to dry (including dessert wines), you can't go wrong with a stop here. (OakCreekVineyards.net)

Alcantara Vineyards

Another dog-friendly vineyard, Alcantara serves a variety of small plates in addition to their wines, which include over 17 varietals of grapes. Alcantara also hosts weddings and other various events. (AlcantaraVineyard.com)

Cottonwood

Cottonwood is a wonderful town nearby Sedona, and like Sedona, it is a vibrant, booming spot. The last few years have seen an explosive growth of activities in Cottonwood, and wineries are just one example. Restaurants have also boomed here, and a favorite to try while sampling the wines is Bocce (BocceCottonwood. com) at 1060 N Main Street. Note, Cottonwood offers tasting rooms, not vineyards, but don't let that stop you from visiting. Cottonwood offers wonderful wine!

AZ Stronghold

AZ Stronghold makes fantastic wines from Arizona-grown grapes, predominantly from Willcox, but also those grown from other areas including the Verde Valley near Sedona. Their Cottonwood tasting room often features wines that cannot be found anywhere else other than their tasting room - so you'll have to stop by to sample! (www.AZStronghold.com)

Pillsbury Wine Company

Not related to the dough boy, Pillsbury Wine Company produces wines from only Arizona-grown grapes from its 80-acre Willcox vineyard. Its Cottonwood tasting room offers a daily happy hour special as well, and though reservations are recommended, they are not required. (PillsburyWine.com)

Provisioner Winery

Owned by AZ Stronghold, Provisioner Winery has its own tasting room. It produces only three wines right now: a white, a blush, and a red. Dubbed as "wine for the people," these affordable wines are a personal favorite of the author and his wife and are routinely one of our go-to daily wines. (AZStronghold.com/ProShop)

Organized Winery Tours

Sip Sedona

These personalized, all-inclusive tours stop at 3-4 local vineyards and include a stop at one of the area's best restaurants to enjoy a meal. (SipSedona.com)

Sedona Wine and Vortex Tours

Private tours that are family-friendly and promise a metaphysical "prana" experience, you'll get exposed to both the vortexes as well as the many wineries in the region. (SedonaWineAndVortexTours.com)

Arizona Winery Tours

Offering shared as well as private tours of three of the Sedona-area wineries, with lunch, bottled water, and all your transportation included (Arizona Winery Tours even picks you up). You'll even get to keep your souvenir tasting glass. (www.ArizonaWineryTours.com)

State Parks & Exploring Outside Sedona

Slide Rock State Park (Sedona, AZ)

Slide Rock, as its name implies, features natural waterslides carved into the rock, all made slick and slippery by the algae that grows on them. Slide Rock State Park is just a short drive up AZ-89A, 5.3 miles from Midgley Bridge (about a 10-minute drive). There is a $20 fee to enter Slide Rock, which rises to $30 per car (1-4 people) between Memorial Day and Labor Day and lowers to $10 from November through February. A $5 per additional person above 4 in a car applies year-round. The annual Red Rock Pass is not accepted here.

Slide Rock's main attraction is the waterslides, which are often quite crowded with children at play in the summer. This is a major draw, and Slide Rock is a very crowded area in the peak season. During weekends it can feel like you're at a beach party, not in quiet Sedona, so plan accordingly. If you want a similar water experience, minus the slides but including cliff jumping, check out Bell Trail (The Crack) in the VOC hiking section. Bell Trail has a longer approach, which cuts back on crowds.

Slide Rock has a few short hiking trails through the park, but this isn't the reason you're visiting Slide Rock. Better hiking can be found elsewhere, though upstream of the water slides and swimming area at Slide Rock can be a great place for anglers in search of a trophy trout.

Jerome Ghost Town (Jerome, AZ)

A popular day-trip for those visiting Sedona, Jerome, Arizona is touted as the liveliest ghost town in America. With an increasing population due to the recent tourism boom, Jerome can hardly be called a ghost town anymore (at least not officially).

Located 45 minutes southwest of Sedona (halfway between Sedona and Prescott, Arizona), it's definitely worth a day's visit to this former copper and gold mining town that once boasted a population upwards of 3,000 people (around the year 1900). Jerome today keeps its old world charm, yet adds modern amenities to give you just a taste of the wild, wild west. You can pan for your own gold in the Gold King Mine and see what life was like for miners when the mine was in its peak. In addition, you can tour the Gold King property, which features over 180 old cars and trucks, all well preserved in the Arizona desert. Reservations for some activities are required. (GoldKingMineGhostTown.com)

Another great option is to check out the Jerome State Historic Park, which features historical exhibits reminiscent of the old mining days of the early 1900's, including furnished living quarters plus a 3D model of the town and its mines.

If you're staying for a meal, check out the Haunted Hamburger. This venue is supposedly haunted, though the story leaves many skeptics doubting the authenticity of the haunt. You can be the judge! (TheHauntedHamburger.com)

Grand Canyon National Park (Tusayan, AZ)

The Grand Canyon seems to be on everyone's bucket list, and although it's worthy of it's own dedicated long weekend trip, it can also be day-tripped from Sedona (or piggy-backed for a few nights). The drive takes about 2 hours from Sedona and is a very easy drive. Arrive early in peak seasons for two reasons: the roads will fill up quickly with slow-moving RV's and it's not always feasible to pass them on the long stretch of two-lane road leading to the South Rim main entrance, and the line to pay for the canyon entrance can also back up for 30+ minutes at times of peak demand. For the best experience, plan to arrive no later than 8:00 in the morning.

The Grand Canyon has quite a few trails to explore, from trails above the rim (which are all dog-friendly, and include paved options as well as off-road) to trails below the rim (not dog-friendly) that offer access to the Colorado River at the bottom, if you have the time and the endurance for this hike.

Contrary to what every sign will tell you, it's possible to hike to the bottom and back up in a single day in good weather, if you are a very strong hiker. You need to ensure you really are a strong desert hiker. Rescue here is not cheap or easy, and unlike your Sedona area hikes, this hike starts with the easy downhill and then challenges you to climb back out, in some cases packing on over 5,000' of elevation, so try it at your own risk! For a mainstream trail experience, complete South Kaibab or Bright Angel Trails, and enjoy the passing mule trains. If you want a quieter hike, Hermit Trail is the quietest, though Grandview Trail is fairly quiet and features Cave of the Domes, the only cave in GCNP open to the public. If hiking to the cave, follow Grandview to the spur trail at GPS 36.026270,-111.980582, then follow the spur to the cave at 36.026851,-111.982971. Round-trip rim to cave is about 7 miles.

The bottom of the Kaibab Trail.

Humphrey's Peak (Flagstaff, AZ)

A trip to Humphrey's Peak will be the high point of your Arizona vacation, quite literally. The tallest peak in Arizona, Humphrey's stands at 12,637' above sea level and is an easily-accessible long yet moderate (steep but non-technical) 10.5 miles round trip hike. Best reserved for the summertime as an escape from the desert heat, be sure to hike it early in the day before the afternoon monsoons have a chance to roll in. Check the weather forecast carefully, as you do not want to get caught in a storm up here, especially above the tree line where the most electrically conductive thing on the mountain is you! If you decide to tackle this hike in the winter or spring, expect snow, and expect a technical ascent (ice axes and crampons, with avalanche danger) and be prepared with proper techniques of self-rescue and self-arrest.

The most common approach to the peak is found by parking in the well-market lower Snowbowl parking lot (GPS 35.330773, -111.711440) and hiking the trail appropriately named "Humphrey's Trail." Snowbowl is the local ski hill, and this hike starts with a quick excursion through the ski slopes and past the lifts, before entering the forest and ascending a series of steep switchbacks to the saddle. A brief hike beyond the saddle crosses the tree line and takes you to the peak, where you'll be treated to panoramic views of the San Francisco Peaks (no relation to the California city - you can't see *that* far), the Grand Canyon, Verde Valley, and Sedona.

Humphrey's Peak is a wonderful climb that should be on your bucket list, but if you're not a frequent visitor to Arizona and have a choice of a day at Humphrey's or a day at the Grand Canyon, I'd usually opt for the Grand Canyon unless it's a very hot summer day. Hiking below the canyon rim in the middle of summer is not fun; on these hot days, Humphrey's makes an equally exciting yet bearable alternative!

Humphrey's Peak during an afternoon thunderstorm.

Sunset Crater National Monument (Flagstaff, AZ)

A very underrated site, Sunset Crater National Monument in Flagstaff is often confused with Meteor Crater Natural Landmark in Winslow, Arizona. The latter is a privately owned tourist attraction where a meteor impact left a large hole in the ground. The former, and our subject of discussion, is a registered national monument that's definitely worth a day's visit and is only about one hour from Sedona.

Sunset Crater itself is a volcanic cinder cone crater created in the year 1085 (quite recently, by Geological standards) and today is a national landmark featuring numerous hiking trails throughout the fairly small park. The result of the catastrophic lava eruption is a dispersal of dark black lava over a field dotting the landscape. Over the nearly 1,000 years since eruption, little has regrown in these dense lava fields, and it makes for a beautiful contrast between the lush forests and barren lava.

This monument is best explored in a single day, and there are quite a few small trails worth hiking here that can all be done back-to-back. Because each trail is quite short, you can travel light. Bring a camera and a small bottle of water. Even in the peak of summer, the higher elevation of this park will keep you fairly cool compared to the lower elevations of the Sedona desert.

Favorite hikes here include a loop around the Lenox Crater Trail (1.6 miles, moderate), the Lava Flow Trail (1 mile, partially paved, easy), and the Lava's Edge Trail (3.4 miles, moderate). There is also O'Leary Peak Trail, which ascents a lava dome (not the Sunset Crater cinder cone) and yields great views into Sunset Crater. The O'Leary Peak Trail is a wide fire road and not a singletrack trail but is one of our favorite for the views. It ends at a firetower that is not on the true summit. Adventurous hikers can push on to the summit.

The view from O'Leary Peak Trail.

Lava River Caves (Flagstaff, AZ)

Flagstaff is chock-full of volcanic activity, and the Lava River Caves are another unique example of the beauty and power of nature. These hollow tubes of lava formed from volcanic flows that ejected from the ground over 700,000 years ago. As it flowed, the outer edge of the lava cooled and hardened while hot gases ejected the molten lava core, leaving behind a hollow tube. The lava tubes can be safely hiked from end to end, which is about 3/4 of a mile one-way. They're perfectly dark from end-to-end, making a surreal experience, so bring a headlamp (plus a backup).

Located 75 minutes from Sedona, these caves are a great excursion to escape the summer heat. The lava tubes can be hiked easily from spring through fall, or approached using cross-country skis in winter (with a longer approach, as the road is not plowed to the end). Regardless of when you visit, the tubes hold a constant 35°F to 40°F, so bring a jacket and some sturdy boots.

To reach the lava tubes, head to the northwest of Flagstaff and park on Fire Rd. 171B (it is best to navigate to GPS coordinates 35.342730, -111.837948). From here, the cave entrance is an easy 1/4-mile approach on a flat, well-worn trail. Exploring the cave takes some very mild rock hopping over uneven terrain and loose boulders, and the cave has a fairly low ceiling in some places, so crouching may be required and a helmet is recommended. On the whole, this is a pretty easy hike and accessible to anyone if good care is exercised.

Petrified Forest National Park (Adamana, AZ)

Located a little over two hours from Sedona, Petrified Forest National Park is another easy day trip from Sedona and offers a fun, unique experience. This park is frequently visited by those driving by on the highway that don't even know it exists until they see the sign and decide to check it out, and the park does a wonderful job of laying out itineraries for a one-hour, few-hour, or half-day visit. There are quite a few short trails that take you to the various viewpoints, which include Native American petroglyphs, various petrified wood remains, and several scenic overlooks. The Painted Desert Rim and Crystal Forest Trails are recommended. Unlike most national parks, Petrified Forest is extremely dog friendly, so bring your pup and enjoy!

A petrified log bridge in Petrified Forest National Park.

Montezuma's Castle / Montezuma's Well (Camp Verde, AZ)

A national monument site dedicated to preserving the history of the Sinagua culture, Montezuma's Castle is best known for the ruins of a 5-story cliff dwelling and the beautiful oasis just up the road (Montezuma's Well) that hosts diverse and unique life.

Montezuma's Castle takes just a few hours to visit and is a quick and convenient 25 minutes from the Village of Oak Creek, just south on I-17 (GPS: 34.610773, -111.837517). Guided tours are also offered, but call ahead or check their website for availability: (928) 567-3322 or www.nps.gov/moca. The Red Rock parking pass is not accepted, but the annual National Parks Pass is. It is not possible to ascend to the ruins; they're too delicate for visitors, but a scale model replica on the trail shows what the inside looks like and details what life was like for the Sinagua people. A short hiking trail navigates you through a few different viewpoints

Montezuma's Well is a sub-unit of Montezuma's Castle National Monument and is detached from the Montezuma's Castle site (it's actually located 11 miles away), making it an easy secondary excursion on your way up to Sedona. Montezuma's Well features a beautiful but short hike into the watering hole, passing along the creek for a bit of a reprieve from the sun on a hot day. A popular birdwatching site, Montezuma's Well is also a great site for observing some unique desert aquatic animals and is a popular watering hole for many desert mammals.

Both sites can be seen in less than a half day starting from Sedona. Their location pairs well with any hike in the VOC, especially the Bell Trail (The Crack), which starts quite close to the entrance to Montezuma's Well.

Montezuma's Castle, built into the cliff side.

Sample Daily Itineraries

Day 1: Village of Oak Creek Area

The VOC offers a great introduction to Sedona. Wake up early, and grab a coffee and snack at Oak Creek Espresso. Take it to go, and drive to Bell Rock Parking, just a minute away. Sip your morning coffee along the flats of Bell Rock Pathway, up to Bell Rock proper (the iconic rock formation to your right). Discard your coffee at the trashcan at Courthouse Vista parking before heading straight up the face of Bell Rock, as far as your comfort allows (you cannot summit without technical gear, but you can scramble quite high). Return back down to terra firma, and continue along Bell Rock Pathway to the split with Baby Bell. Follow Baby Bell Trail to a well-worn use trail up the top of this small formation and gain the mini-summit to enjoy the views. Return to your car via the Rector Trail, following it between Courthouse Butte and Bell Rock, to Big Park Loop back to Bell Rock Pathway and to your car.

By now, you're 2 - 3 hours in and probably starting to think about lunch. Drive over to Clark's Market, pick up some picnic items and a small blanket, and head back to Bell Rock Parking Area. Park, then exit and walk straight across the main Hwy-179 and find the use trail that connects to Slim Shady Trail. Follow it a short way to the sandstone monoliths on the left side, walk up the monoliths (a gentle Class 2 scramble at worst), and enjoy your picnic with some beautiful views over Yavapai Vista without worrying about crowds to disturb your meal. You may very well be alone here.

After lunch, dodge the heat of the day by checking out some of the art galleries in the VOC (weekends usually feature an art festival somewhere in the Village), then prepare for a short but enjoyable hike to Chicken Point via Little Horse Trail. It'll be much quieter at this time of day. Gain the views of Chicken Point, return how you came, and go grab a low-key dinner at Tortas de Fuego, found right on Hwy-179/Jacks Canyon, or a more elaborate upscale dinner at Cucina Rustica (in the Collective on Hwy-179).

This day should wake up your legs and open up your lungs if you're not used to the Sedona elevation (which is quite moderate, but can be noticeable for those coming from sea level), but it should leave you feeling energized and refreshed rather than exhausted. This is an easy day's worth of work, but you'll enjoy much of the beautiful sights that the VOC has to offer, as well as the delicious food. Finish your day with ice cream from Rocky Road Ice Cream (in the Collective on Hwy 179).

Day 2: Uptown

Today we're shopping and eating, but we'll burn off those calories with some short hikes in between. Start with breakfast at the Secret Garden Cafe in the Tlaquepaque Village, then drive south down Morgan Rd. to the parking lot for Broken Arrow Trail. Hike around here as long as you want (the Twin Butte, High on the Hog, Broken Arrow loop is recommended). Check out the sinkhole on Broken Arrow, or you can even hike around the totality of the Twin Buttes rock formation and to the Chapel of the Holy Cross (see the Little Horse Trail description).

When you're done, drive back Uptown (either back to Tlaquepaque or to Uptown proper), park, and walk the busy strip. Hit the shops and grab yourself some lunch. If you're Uptown, stop at Pink Jeep and book yourself a tour for tomorrow or the next day. The best is the jeep tour to Chicken Point, but if you've already followed this guide and hiked Broken Arrow on foot, don't hesitate to try a new place.

While in town, check out the kitschy souvenir shops and grab a good luck crystal. Even if you're a non-believer, I'm told the crystal magic still works. When you're shopped out, grab lunch Uptown at Wildflower, then head further up 89-A. Depending on how much time you have, hike Wilson Mountain or AB Young (some of Sedona's longest, steepest trails), West Fork (shorter, a classic), The Hangover, or Sterling Pass to Vultee Arch and back. If time and energy allows before dinner, swing by Slide Rock State Park, or hike to the nearby Grasshopper Point via the Midgley Bridge Trail and soak your feet in Oak Creek (always cold, even in the peak of summer) until they're either feeling refreshed or just plain numb. Return to town and grab some low-key food at Javelina Cantina (a pet-friendly spot).

Left: Chicken Point. Below: Midgley Bridge viewed from the Hangover Trail.

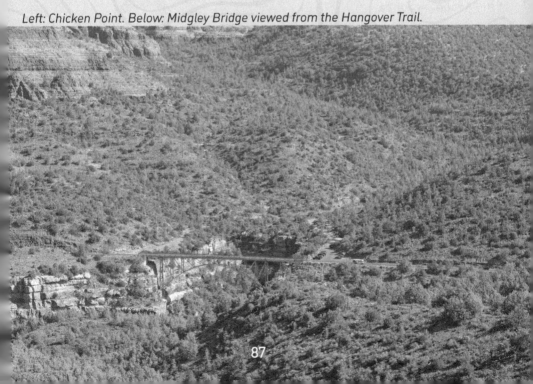

Day 3: West Sedona

Today we're packing on some miles, and you'll get the best of the best for Sedona hiking. I hope you slept well; we're heading up Bear Mountain! Start by 8am for the best access to parking, and prepare to get your elevation on. Bear Mountain isn't technically difficult, but the steep elevation gain is relentless, and a false-summit before the true summit does crush your morale a bit if you're tired (the false summit is really only about the half-way point). Gain the true summit, enjoy the views, and descend Bear Mountain.

Stop by your car, grab some water and a light snack (maybe a trail beer if you're so inclined), and then head straight up Doe Mountain. Doe is quite steep (less so than Bear Mountain), but it's very short, so you can safely ignore your leg's complaints knowing the pain will be short-lived. Gain the summit, walk around, and check out the views.

After descending Doe Mountain, you'll be ready for some lunch. Pisa Lisa is a top choice, and their Funghi Decadente pizza and gelato is to die for. Don't eat too much though, as you'll need your energy for Boynton Canyon. The afternoon here will still be quite crowded, but a bit less so than an early-morning hike. Park in the lot if you're lucky (or on the road otherwise) and hike Boynton Trail. Be sure to check out the Subway Cave (see the Boynton Canyon Trail hiking section for details) before continuing to the end of the hiking trail. Enjoy the views of this beautiful canyon before doubling back to your car. Your legs are probably toast by now, but if it's not quite dinnertime yet, you can stop at Red Rock State Park and take a short stroll to Oak Creek and soak your feet in the chilly river water. Or, depending on the sunset time, you can check out the beautiful sunset from the Airport Mesa overlook before (or after) dinner. Head to dinner at Mariposa in West Sedona, and enjoy the scenic views of the Adobe Jack area.

Boynton Canyon's Subway Cave entrance (the dark, shadowed spot just right of center).

Day 4: Mountain Biking

Saddle up (not your horse, but your full-suspension mountain bike). If you don't have one, don't worry, there's a few rental shops in town. I recommend Thunder Mountain Bikes in West Sedona (ThunderMountainBikes.com), but if you're down in the VOC to start, you can check out Absolute Bikes (AbsoluteBikes.net).

If you only get one day to bike, and you want to make it a long one, ride the West Sedona area (see the *Mountain Biking* section for maps and details). Park along Dry Creek Road at the start of the Lizardhead Trail. Follow that to ChuckWagon, then loop around ChuckWagon to the Mescal Trail (you can follow all of this from the *Dry Creek Road Trails* section under Mountain Biking). From Mescal Trail, make an entire lap around Mescal Mountain (via Deadman's Pass to Long Canyon), then repeat the start, this time dropping into Canyon of Fools and enjoying the jumpline.

Hit Dawa, then follow to Cockscomb and Aerie, for the beautiful Tour de Sedona. If your legs allow it, you can connect into any level of trail you'd like in the Cultural Park area, ride until you're exhausted, then come out at Two Fence Trail. You'll be right near your car. Go grab yourself a well-deserved lunch (or, if you had an especially epic ride, an even more deserved dinner). Carry plenty of water on this day; there isn't really anyplace to stop along the route.

If you prefer to stay in the VOC and bike (preferred if renting from Absolute Bikes), no worries! You can have just as much fun! Leave Absolute Bike's parking lot (on bike, not in your car) and hop onto Bell Rock Pathway for an easy warm up. Head to Baby Bell, then turn onto Llama Trail. Follow Llama up to Little Horse, and then choose your adventure from here. Those seeking tougher riding can follow the two double-blacks High on the Hog and Hog Heaven, finishing up with the fast and flowy jumpline Pigtail. Return to Little Horse via Mystic to the road to Chapel Trail. For those looking for less technical riding, follow Broken Arrow or Twin Butte, then climb back up Hog Wash to Mystic, and return to Little Horse via Chapel.

From here, enjoy the fun descent all the way down Little Horse to Bell Rock Pathway (passing Llama where you first started), then cross the bridge to link to the HT Trail, pass under Hwy 179, and meet up with the Yavapai Vista trails. Ride Templeton to the intersection with Cathedral Rock. If desired, lock up your bike and ascend Cathedral Rock on foot (you're already halfway up, plus you'll avoid the parking mess here). Return back down Templeton to Slim Shady, and power out this super-fun black diamond from north to south. Follow it back to the road, and you'll pop out about 1/4 mile from Absolute Bikes. Return your bike and go find some food!

When you're done with the biking, hop in your car and drive to Sedona Caves (aka Raven Caves). Bring some snacks and a hammock if you're so inclined. This 10-minute hike passes the interesting caves, so stop for a photo, then continue down to the river. Hang your hammock, enjoy your snacks, and enjoy a cold drink. Sunbathe on the river rocks, then return to your car and get some well-earned rest.

Day 5: Flagstaff

We'll venture past Sedona today, and tackle a few attractions in Flagstaff. Start early and head to Snowbowl. No hiking trip in Arizona is complete without getting to the top of the world (or at least, the top of the state), Humphrey's Peak, located a whopping 12,633 feet above sea level. You'll need an early start, as it's a 60-minute drive and the mountain is known for frequent afternoon monsoons, so you want to be down before noon if possible (plan 5+ hours round-trip for the 11-mile hike). The photo below shows a monsoon brewing, and descending through it was not enjoyable. We had welts from the hail!

When you're done with this hike, take the 50-minute drive to Sunset Crater National Monument, and ponder how two locations only a few miles apart can be so vastly different. If your legs just don't want to carry you on any more hikes after Humphrey's Peak, skip the monument and check out the Lowell Observatory, Riordan Mansion Historic Park, or the historic downtown district instead, where you can peruse the various shops and restaurants.

Around nightfall, head over to the Lava River Caves. This is located close to Humphrey's Trailhead, so you'll have some backtracking to do from Sunset Crater. Since they're always pitch black, you don't need to rely on daylight to hike the lava tubes, so visiting in the evening lets you see them without wasting daylight. These tubes take about two hours to hike to the end, explore, and photograph, though the expedient traveler can do it in about an hour. If this is just too much hiking for you, check out Brix Restaurant and Wine Bar, or grab a tour (and a pint) at Flagstaff Brewing Company, Wanderlust Brewing Co, or Mother Road Brewing Co.

If you have a particularly hot day in Sedona (100° or higher), you can expect Flagstaff won't exceed 80°, and it can even be much cooler than this, so bring a jacket. Flagstaff makes for a great escape from the desert heat!

Day 6: Relaxation & Vortexes

If you've followed this so far, you've pounded out some serious mileage, and today is a zero day! Well, maybe not zero, but you'll certainly enjoy some low mileage and relaxation. Start off with a wonderful breakfast at Sedona Crepes, then hit one of the many spas. Sedona's New Day Spa (SedonaNewDaySpa.com) or Amara Resort and Spa (AmaraResort.com/Spa) are great options, and appointments are required for both.

Your massage or other spa treatment should relax you enough to open you to the power of the vortex. Today, we'll keep it close and explore the Airport Mesa vortex, a masculine energy vortex. If you're feeling ambitious, you can hike the entire Airport Loop, but a short 5-minute or less excursion to the lookout is all that's needed to feel the positive energy. Bring a blanket or a yoga mat, a picnic lunch, bottle of wine, or a few beers, and relax and enjoy some of the easiest 360-panoramic views of the wilderness, Uptown, and the beautiful red rock formations of the VOC.

When you've thoroughly recharged your batteries, prepare to saddle up, this time on a real horse instead of a mountain bike. And yes, there will be wine. Check out Horseback Wine Country at Alcantara Vineyards (HorsebackWineCountry.com), where you can actually ride through the vineyards on this beginner-friendly guided tour. From here, hit the tasting room, and if you weren't already relaxed from the massage and horseback ride, just let yourself melt away with the wonderful Arizona wines!

If you're not into horses, opt for a private wine tour, where you'll have the opportunity to hit even more vineyards. Stop over in historic Cottonwood, Arizona and check out the busy Main Street. There are quite a few tasting rooms here, as well as some wonderful restaurants, such as Bocce. Continue on to Jerome, Arizona (only 15 minutes from Cottonwood) and spend the rest of your day here exploring the various haunts, museums, and more.

Head back to Sedona in time to catch a sunset and a lazy evening stroll on Bell Rock Pathway, one of the flattest, easiest trails in the area. Extend it if desired on the equally flat Courthouse Butte Loop. Bring your headlamp and stay out past dark. If you're lucky, you'll be treated to a viewing of the various animals you don't often see in the daytime hours, including rabbits, deer, javelinas, coyotes, and more.

Bring your camera and tripod, and take advantage of Sedona's International Dark Sky Community rating with some wonderful, relaxing astrophotography. If you're here in summer, you can catch the Milky Way band. Not sure what you're looking at? Download any of the best stargazing apps that use augmented reality (Star Walk, SkyView, or Google Sky) or check out TheSkyLive.com to see a list of what's visible when you're in town, and more importantly, what equipment you'll need to see it.

You'll need very long exposures to catch it all on your camera, and to kill time between all those shutter clicks, bring a blanket and a bottle of wine. This is one of my favorite and most romantic ways to end a vacation to Sedona, and amazingly, you'll likely find you're the only one out on the trail. Enjoy this moment!

Conclusion

I hope you've enjoyed this guide, but much more importantly, I hope you enjoy Sedona! I encourage you to make the most of your time in Sedona, but also to branch out to the surrounding areas and make the most of your time in Arizona as a whole. It's a great state with many amazing things to see and do, any time of year!

I also hope I've inspired you to explore a few hikes or visit a few sights that you weren't originally planning to visit, and that I've given you a few pointers to help facilitate your easy travel. Unless you have an extended visit, you won't see everything you want to, but I hope I've helped you prioritize your hit-list and make the most of the time you do have. You can always come back!

I have one final favor to ask. I'm an independent author, and book reviews help me tremendously to continue to develop great content for you! If you can spare a few minutes, please leave this book a review on Amazon, GoodReads, Bookish, LibraryThing, or any other site where you get your book information. I really appreciate it!

I hope to see you on the trails in Sedona soon!

Made in the USA
Las Vegas, NV
19 September 2023

77835644R10057